RECLAIMING
LIVES

RECLAIMING LIVES

PURSUING JUSTICE FOR SIX INNOCENT MEN

JOAN TREPPA

Joan Treppa
8501 Cottagewood Terrace
Minneapolis, MN 55434
© 2017 by Joan Treppa

Printed in the United States of America

ISBN-13: 978-0-99841-420-1

This book is dedicated to those who've suffered in prison due to false convictions, and to those who've stepped in to selflessly help them.

FOREWORD

While at the James River Paper Mill on the morning of November 21, 1992, Tom Monfils disappeared from his work area and was later found dead at another location in the mill. Despite the evidence pointing to suicide, the police assumed an "angry mob" of his coworkers had murdered him. The investigation soon centered on six men who had been working at the mill that day. I know this because I am one of those six.

Few people, unless they or someone close to them has experienced what the "Monfils Six" and their families have endured, are likely to understand the anxiety and sense of helplessness that overtakes an innocent person while he cooperates with law enforcement, only to have it call him a liar, a thug, and a murderer. Few can know what an innocent person suffers as he loses his job and becomes the subject of media stories and public contempt for a crime he did not commit. They will not experience or know the frustration an innocent person experiences watching his family suffer as the investigation and trial continue.

Most people assume, as I once did, that even if the police and prosecutors do not know or admit the truth, the jury will surely find it in the end. In the "Monfils Six" case, like in other wrongful conviction cases, this did not happen. All six of us were convicted of first-degree intentional homicide, sentenced to life in prison, and separated from our families and everything else that made our lives worthwhile. From then on, we could only hope that someday the truth would become clear and the injustice corrected. Our days would be filled with the depression, despair, and disappointment that an innocent man endures as his appeals and other legal efforts fail, and he fears he will never regain his freedom and life.

Staying hopeful is difficult. Because I have been convicted, the struggle is uphill. That is something every wrongfully convicted person soon learns. What I have also learned is that an innocent person can choose to maintain his own integrity. It is one thing the system cannot take. I will continue to speak the truth and declare my innocence, just as the other members of the "Monfils Six" have.

After I had been in prison for more than fifteen years, I received a letter from Joan Treppa, a woman I had never met, but whose life was also changed by this case. She became a champion for all of us and for all wrongfully convicted people. If we regain our freedom, it will be because Joan cared and acted when she saw an injustice. I hope this book inspires others to follow her path and become advocates for the wrongfully convicted. –Keith M. Kutska

INTRODUCTION

I n December of 2015 I met a prison inmate named Dale Basten at the Stanley Correctional Institution in Stanley, Wisconsin. At the current age of seventy-seven, he's the oldest of six men convicted of murder in the 1992 death of a paper mill worker named Tom Monfils. I always enjoyed letters from Dale. They were infrequent and short but full of genuine warmth, sincerity, and honesty.

In the prison lounge at Stanley, my husband, Mike, and I sat waiting for Dale to come through the door at the far end of the room. The procedure was to check in with the prison guard and then join us at our designated table, number 18. As we waited we eyed an elderly inmate being escorted into the lounge by a prison guard. I was saddened by this procession as the man shuffled past our table with the guard following close behind, holding on to his arm for support. It was only after they'd passed by when we realized it was Dale. I immediately jumped up and peeked around the corner as they approached the guard desk. Dale checked in and turned to face the crowded room. He looked terribly confused. The guard patiently waited for Dale to locate his visitors. They both scanned the room for visible signs of acknowledgment. When one of them glanced in our direction, I waved them over. Dale headed toward us but only at the urging of the guard. Dale was thin and appeared frail. I thought he might trip, so I braced myself, watching for any signs of him falling forward. The guard left Dale with us and we assisted him into his designated seat—the maroon chair sitting amid three others that were a deep shade of green. Dale looked at us and offered a cordial smile. It was obvious he had no idea who we were, even though I had sent him regular updates and letters for the past five years.

"How are you doing, Dale?" I asked. He shrugged and said, "I'm fine." He then said he'd never been in this room before. Mike and I looked at each other. We were thinking the same thing. This was improbable because Dale had been at this prison at least since 2009, and we knew his family had visited during that time. Maybe he just didn't remember. We kept our questions simple in case he was experiencing memory problems. We asked about everyday life at the prison. Dale's answers were short. His recollection of current activities was vague. But clarity resurfaced somewhat when we asked him about things of the distant past, like the incident at the paper mill in 1992.

Dale told us he was a foreman at the mill. He said he liked his job and that his income provided a good life for his family. He told us he didn't work in the area of the mill where the incident occurred, but that he and Mike Johnson had been called there to help with one of the paper machines during the morning of Tom Monfils' disappearance. Dale obsessed over his interpretation of how Monfils' body reacted while in the vat. Numerous times with his arms, he recreated a swirling, plunging motion as he narrated.

Dale did not recall his parole hearing a month prior to this visit. There was, however, recollection and no mistaking his love for his two daughters, despite being able to recall few details of their current lives. Mike and I were conscious of the fact that Dale might be experiencing symptoms similar to what my elderly mother experienced late in life—short-term memory loss, vague recollections of current events, and an inability to retain new information, no matter how significant. After this visit I spoke with Dale's brother, Lee. Lee commented on how much Dale had aged in prison and how Dale's health had advanced ten years beyond his actual age due to inadequate health care, a lack of human touch, and constant exposure to his high-stress situation. Dale's current state had most likely intensified from a major health concern he dealt with a few years ago. I'm not aware of the complete details but I learned Dale had suffered a major heart attack. No one in the family was told about this when it happened and when they did find out, prison staff wouldn't offer details about his condition. It sent the family into panic mode when they were not permitted to be with Dale during this critical time.

Witnessing Dale's age-related challenges that day prompted me to research information about the aging prison population in the US. According to Human Rights Watch, due to the "get tough on crime" initiative years ago, which caused longer prison sentences for lesser crimes, an overwhelming number of aging inmates are now adding to the overcrowding within prisons today. The number of men and women aged fifty-five–plus years has grown dramatically, from roughly 32,600 in 1995 to 124,400 in 2010. That's an increase of 282 percent in comparison with a 42.1 percent increase in the total prison population during the same years. In 2000, elderly inmates accounted for only 3 percent of the total prison population. In just ten years, their numbers increased by 5 percent. Now they account for approximately 16 percent of the total prison population. Projections estimate the aging prison population may increase by 4,400 percent based on statistics from 1981 to 2030. With this forecast, by 2030, prisoners fifty-five and over will reach one-third of the total prison population.

There is a major concern about cost and physical care required during their incarceration period. Prison staff is ill equipped to take on such duties. And, although there are plenty of senior care facilities in this country, the problem lies with sending aged prisoners to these facilities, which causes safety concerns for residents and staff members. Since we met him, Dale's family has been unable to find appropriate housing outside of the prison system. As a temporary measure, Dale was recently transferred to a maximum security prison equipped with the necessary medical care he needs. Fortunately, he's being held in a section of the prison separate from the general population.

I learned about Dale's situation in 2009, from a book called *The Monfils Conspiracy: The Conviction of Six Innocent Men*; a story I found deeply disturbing about a real-life tragedy that has upset Dale's life and the lives of countless others. Reading about their difficulties affected me to the core, like a jab to the heart that has never diminished since. I could not accept nor dismiss this depiction of a criminal court case that developed into a horrific injustice and prime example of the widespread deficiencies that result in wrongful convictions. The concept of being wrongfully convicted was foreign to me, but what captured my attention was a perceived element of bullying as the underlying theme in this case. Bullying was something my childhood was inundated with. Bullies had made fun of me, defamed my character, blamed me for things I didn't do until my mental state was reduced to feelings of shame and self-pity. As an adult, and after a long road to restoring my self-esteem, I read those same iniquities in this book.

The story details the flaws of the case, which the authors claim led a jury to convict six innocent men. They described circumstances well beyond what I had experienced—authorities unlawfully fabricating evidence to secure lifelong prison sentences. As I read further into the book I realized how insignificant my past was, but also, how much it mattered. I could empathize with these individuals on a fundamental level because of what I went through, which is why I felt compelled to help defend them and their rights. My most effective tool became my personal tragedies, which motivated me to act with a strong and steady passion. After a while, this Good Samaritan crusade turned into an important lesson in self-discovery, in achieving a more meaningful life, and learning that hope is the most powerful emotion we will ever experience.

The backdrop of this story centers on events that took place in the Midwest section of the United States, in the city of Green Bay, Wisconsin. The body of Tom Monfils was found inside a pulp vat at a local paper mill where he worked. A questionable investigation followed and its outcome became a bitter pill for all its victims to swallow. The book touches lightly on the technical and legal aspects of the case. However, the majority of this story comes from the standpoint of a citizen advocate who has no legal background, only a fierce determination to be one of the many voices for those silenced. My preference for being labeled an advocate, as opposed to an activist, stems from feeling more comfortable working behind the scenes, allowing the real heroes to shine in the foreground.

It wasn't my intention to write a book when I first started down this path, so the book's content is based on memory, conversations with the people involved in the case, e-mails, blog posts, other documentation I saved over the years, and more recent legal briefs. Although I've taken some liberty regarding dialogue and circumstances, I've done my best to capture the essence of what was either said or done in the events depicted throughout this book. Some names have been changed for privacy. Conversations with certain persons have been intentionally left out due to attorney-client privilege and because the case is currently going through a lengthy litigation process.

Despite strong opposing views, I've ample reasons, many of which I address in this book, to believe that Dale and the other five men convicted in this case are innocent. But I don't expect those who read my book to readily accept the content I've provided solely on its merits. To further understand the complexities and specifics of this case, I urge you to read *The Monfils Conspiracy* book and perform your own in-depth examination of this and other wrongful conviction cases which have grown in number and gained widespread attention across the country. Thank you for taking the time to read about this one.

1

HOMEGROWN SECRETS

"What do you mean there are innocent people in prison?" I asked. "How is that possible?"

John replied, "Let me explain."

In a phone conversation with my sister Clare during the summer of 2009, she described someone she'd met recently. "He's an author and researcher named John Gaie," she said. "We met at a place called The Lorelei. And get this, he told me I look like his mother."

We laughed. Clare and John are longtime residents of Green Bay. They'd been dating for a few weeks before Clare asked about bringing John to Minnesota to meet my husband Mike and me. She was anxious for us to hear about a project he was working on. "John is researching a true crime story I am familiar with," she said. "He's working with two other people on a book about six men who were convicted of murder in 1995, right here in Green Bay. John says it will be published soon."

"No kidding," I said. "That's exciting. I've always been interested in true crime stories. I'd love to hear more about this one."

Concern in Clare's voice indicated her deep distress over the circumstances and the outcome. It wasn't until I heard her next statements that I became aware of the degree to which this case affected both of them. "I'll let John speak for himself about his connection, but I'll say this for now. Both of us have direct ties to this case. John's connection compelled him to take on this book project and do most of the research. In the process he found

1

many flaws with the entire case that I didn't know about. I always felt there was something terribly wrong with how it turned out and I'm even more convinced of that now. Plus, I know one of the convicted men. Rey Moore is a good friend of mine," she said. She touched on bits and pieces of how she'd gotten to know Rey. "I worked with Rey's wife for many years at the county," she said. "When she introduced me to Rey the three of us ended up hanging out together on many occasions."

I wanted to hear so much more but we decided to wait until they came to our house to visit. "When can you and John drive over?" I asked.

"We'll come the weekend after next. It'll be fun," she said.

2

TRAGEDY IN TITLETOWN, USA

C lare and John arrived early Friday evening, in time for dinner. Clare introduced us to a man whose grin was mischievous and sly, reminiscent of the Cheshire cat. But he was friendly and outgoing, with a boisterous and infectious laugh. His slight build did not prevent him from giving bear hugs that forced the air out of our lungs, and compliments from him seemed to flow naturally. "You're almost as beautiful as your sister," John said.

"And you're quite the charmer," I replied.

John was retired. He talked about his career as a scientist and researcher who taught biochemistry for twenty-five years at Northwest Wisconsin Technical College. He shared his love of teaching and of being among innovative students. We soon learned every conversation with John turned into a fifty-five-minute lecture. Nevertheless, he accommodated us when we'd interrupt him with remarks of our own on the given topic. Talk during dinner was relaxed and full of laughter, but the mood turned somber when I changed the subject as we moved into the family room.

"Tell us about the book you are working on," I said.

John was eager to share the story. "The book is called *The Monfils Conspiracy: The Conviction of Six Innocent Men*. I'm a coauthor with Denis Gullickson, a local Green Bay writer who has written two books about the Green Bay Packers." In a calm, subdued manner, John shared vast details of an intolerable and heartbreaking story that, to him, was still unresolved seventeen years later.

His narrative started out with a seemingly mundane event that occurred on November 10, 1992, and turned catastrophic over a period of two and a half years. While at work at the James River Paper Mill in Green Bay, mill worker Keith Kutska cut a sixteen-foot piece of electrical wire from an area in the mill containing discarded scrap materials, intending to take it home with him at the end of his shift. Typically, mill employees were permitted to take scrap items home with them, but they were required to fill out a "scrap pass" so that management could keep track of which items were being removed for personal use. Nonetheless, Kutska decided he was going to take the wire without securing the pass because the wire had nominal value and it was common practice within the mill to ignore this directive.

A coworker, Tom Monfils, saw Kutska cut the wire. At that time, he and Kutska knew they were on opposite sides of a local union vote proposal. Because of this, Monfils may have intended to make trouble for Kutska. So on the day Kutska took the wire, Monfils made an anonymous 911 call to the Green Bay Police Department (GBPD) to report Kutska's impending theft of the wire. During the call he told the police that he wanted to remain anonymous because Kutska was "violent" and a "biker type" even though, as the police later learned, Kutska had no history of violence. Monfils requested the police go to the mill, presumably to arrest Kutska. Instead, the 911 dispatcher called mill security to report the impending theft and Kutska was stopped by a guard when leaving work after his shift was over. Kutska was asked to open his bag but he refused. The following day there was a disciplinary hearing for Kutska at the mill. He denied taking the wire, as directed by the local union president, who said Kutska would have a better chance of keeping his job if he did not admit to taking it. Kutska was ultimately suspended from work for five days.

At the disciplinary hearing, Kutska learned the police had received an anonymous call from one of his coworkers on the same day as he had taken the wire. He also learned copies of these 911 call recordings were obtainable by the public. Word later traveled throughout the mill about Kutska's intent to discover who had made the call. Distraught over the realization his deed could be exposed, Monfils made repeated phone calls to the police, asking them not to release the recording. At the same time Monfils was reassured they would not release it, others in the police department helped Kutska to obtain the recording.

On November 20, Kutska drove to the police station and secured a copy of the recording. He paid a fee of five dollars and replaced the copy he received with a blank cassette tape. After listening to the recording, Kutska immediately recognized the voice as Monfils. He then played it for the local union president, who advised him to play the tape at work on the following morning in the presence of Monfils and two witnesses. The union president told Kutska, if Monfils admitted it was his voice on the tape, Kutska could then file a union grievance and expose Monfils as a snitch.

On November 21, at about 7:15 a.m., Kutska confronted Monfils with the recording with two of his coworkers present, Mike Piaskowski and Randy LePak. Monfils was stunned to hear the recording but he admitted to Kutska that it was his voice on the tape and that he had reported Kutska to the police. Kutska, Piaskowski, and LePak then left the room, leaving Monfils alone.

Kutska immediately called the union president to say he had what he needed to file the grievance. He then proceeded to play the tape for other mill workers in the area.

Also during that time, Monfils returned to his work station and performed various tasks on his paper machine. He completed them by 7:40 a.m. At approximately 7:45 a.m., Monfils disappeared from his station. His absence triggered a search for him by mill management and his coworkers.

The following evening, on November 22, 1992, Tom Monfils' body was found at the bottom of a paper pulp vat in the mill. The vat held some twenty thousand gallons of water and pulp particles and was equipped with large rotating propeller blades that were attached on the inside vat wall. One end of Monfils' own jump rope was tied around his neck and the other end was tied to the handle of a forty-nine-pound weight.

Rescuers possibly caused damage to the body by attempting, many times without success, to hoist it up and out of the vat before deciding to remove it through an access portal near the bottom of the vat. As the body flowed out of the portal, so did potential evidence, much of it most likely vanishing through the drainage system. The GBPD also neglected to cordon off the area with crime tape, allowing officers and mill workers alike to trample through the area all day long. Even a police officer's jacket was left carelessly draped on a ladder attached to the side of the vat.

The forensic pathologist assigned to the case began her autopsy examination of Monfils' body on November 23, some forty-two hours after police believed he became submerged in the vat liquid. By that time, the body was in a state of advanced decomposition, bloated and discolored, rendering it unrecognizable. The body had sustained many injuries, including a significant skull fracture. The pathologist rejected any possibility of this being a suicide and determined on the basis of her autopsy that Monfils had been beaten with one or more blunt objects and, while still alive, placed in the vat where he drowned.

Following the autopsy, GBPD sergeant Randy Winkler, who eventually became the lead detective on the case, theorized after Monfils disappeared from sight at around 7:45 a.m., that Kutska and others confronted him near a water bubbler (fountain) where they verbally harassed him before brutally beating him. Winkler also theorized in order to conceal their bloody attack, they tied a weight to Monfils' own jump rope and carried him to the vat to dispose of his body. Winkler also assumed there were multiple witnesses to this altercation.

But many of Monfils' fellow mill workers who knew him were certain he'd committed suicide. They told the police Monfils had psychological problems, an obsession with death and dying, had frequently made remarks about the many drowned suicide victims he'd recovered (with heavy objects tied to their bodies) while serving in the coast guard, and was the subject of rumors about his failed marriage. One mill worker told police Monfils was "ingenious" and "the type of person who'd kill himself and make it look like someone else had done it." Another said Monfils "fully understood the need to tie the weight to his body in order to overcome the instinctive resistance of a conscious person to drowning himself."

About twenty-five minutes after Kutska had played the tape for him, Monfils was seen by a coworker heading toward an entrance to a coop (small breakroom) where the weight (that was used) was sitting on the floor. Nearby was a storage area where Monfils' jump rope hung on a railing. This worker assumed Monfils would enter the coop, which was occupied by other workers. Monfils never did so. The logical conclusion suggests he picked up the rope and weight and walked unseen toward an isolated area of the mill, to the vat where he took his own life.

When Winkler and other detectives on the case found no one to confirm their homicide theory, they presumed a union-inspired "conspiracy of silence" was in place to protect the murderers. Winkler resolved to employ interrogation and other tactics to overcome this "obstruction" and validate his homicide theory. He began to threaten mill workers, subjecting them to an atmosphere of fear and intimidation. They were told they were either "a witness or a suspect," that they could be tried for first-degree intentional homicide, be arrested for obstructing justice, and lose their jobs if they didn't "cooperate" with police. Cooperation meant telling the police they had seen what police wanted them to say they had seen.

Because the forensic pathologist determined Monfils had bled profusely from his beating injuries, the police searched the mill for blood or trace evidence of the presumed attack. Despite a search that included the use of black lights and luminol, they found no such evidence or attempts to remove, destroy, or conceal it. They failed to locate blunt objects matching the size and dimensions of Monfils' alleged injuries. No trace evidence, other physical evidence, and/or eyewitness testimony ever directly corroborated the homicide theory.

Winkler did learn that after Kutska confronted Monfils with the tape, Monfils saw the looks, the finger-pointing, and heard condemnation aimed at him from coworkers. Tom had damaged the Monfils name at the mill where his father and other family members had spent their careers. His wife answered affirmatively when asked if her husband was capable of harming himself after he had admitted reporting Kutska to the police. Her own search for her husband led her to visit local hospitals and a psychiatric facility.

Another interesting fact that surfaced while researching the book was that in early 1994, the six defendants were called in to take polygraph tests. Some of them experienced deliberate disruptions during those tests. One of the six, Mike Johnson, recalls hearing a sudden racket from behind immediately after the administrator of the test asked him this question: "Did you have anything to do with the murder of Tom Monfils?" Johnson had turned around to see Winkler pounding on the window of the room yelling, "Now we gotcha!" in an effort to skew the results. But in the end, none of the men flunked their lie detector tests.

A group of nine men were initially targeted as the main suspects in the investigation but that list was later reduced to include Dale Basten, Mike Hirn, Mike Johnson, Keith Kutska, Reynold Moore, and Mike Piaskowski. The theory by law enforcement claimed these six men allegedly participated in the beating and drowning of Tom Monfils. These men were openly surveilled by the police, with squad cars often spotted near their homes. Officers also rummaged through garbage cans at their homes. The men were asked to go to the police station for questioning on multiple occasions. Even though all of them fully cooperated, they were still characterized by the police and the media as "murderers" and "union thugs".

On April 12, 1995, arrests were made some two and a half years after the body was discovered. The state formally charged the six men with first-degree intentional homicide and two others with misdemeanors. They were held in the Brown County jail. On Thursday, April 13, the Green Bay *Press-Gazette* reported, "Police wrapped up a lengthy investigation in a 45-minute drama in which five mill workers were led out of the mill in handcuffs. Four teams of eight officers swooped in on the mill, and other locations to arrest eight men." Michael Piaskowski recalls being summoned to his supervisor's office and upon entering, being thrown against the wall and handcuffed in a dramatic scene as though he were highly dangerous and a flight risk. The fact was, he and seven others were in the midst of carrying out their typical daily routines.

The six defendants went on trial in late September of 1995. Each of them testified. All of them denied any involvement in or knowledge of the murder. They were tried jointly but each had his own defense attorney, all of whom failed to consider the suicide angle, leaving them with no other choice than to redirect blame away from their client and toward the possible guilt of other men using what is commonly referred to as the SODDI (Some Other Dude Did It) defense. They conceded the prosecution's theory that Monfils had been beaten and drowned by union thugs caught up in the moment. The prosecution set low expectations when it told the jury at the beginning of the trial, "If details are extremely important to you, you're going to be disappointed. There are gaps." In addition to the testimony of the forensic pathologist, the state relied mainly on the testimony of three key witnesses: Brian Kellner, David Weiner, and James Gilliam.

In November 1994, months before the trial started, mill worker Brian Kellner became a witness for the prosecution. Through intimidation, manipulation, and threats, Kellner was coerced into signing a false statement about an alleged role-playing reenactment of the alleged beating at the mill. This incident supposedly took place at the Fox Den Bar, located twenty miles north of Green Bay. According to Kellner's statement, Kutska reenacted the beating after drinking heavily at the bar. The owners of the bar adamantly denied any such event had ever occurred, but Kellner's reenactment statement was hailed as critical by the authorities because it helped to revive an investigation that was heading nowhere.

Before trial, Kellner attempted to retract and change aspects of his statement. After trial, he gave an altered version of the statement. About sixteen months later, he testified he had lied at trial. Now, he said Kutska had not described an actual beating, but had only described what might have happened if the police theory was correct. Kellner said Winkler threatened to have him fired and have his children taken away if he did not sign a statement incriminating the six men. The authorities, in turn, argued Kellner's recantation was not credible.

Another mill worker, David Weiner, whose work station was near the vat, also became a witness for the prosecution. He initially confirmed Kutska's whereabouts at the time of the alleged beating. He also said he didn't see anything relevant to Monfils' disappearance and expressly denied seeing Dale Basten and Michael Johnson that morning. Weiner was later told by district attorney John Zakowski that he was lying and was being considered as a suspect.

Two months after Zakowski told him this, Weiner was at a wedding reception where he was drinking heavily. He became distraught and called the police about a previously "repressed memory" he now recalled of seeing Basten and Johnson bent over as though they were carrying something heavy and walking in the direction of the pulp vat. Although he was not certain about what the object being carried was, authorities presumed it was Monfils' body. As the Monfils trial approached in 1995, Weiner was in prison for killing his own brother and was looking to cut a deal—less time served in exchange for his testimony. None of this was ever disclosed to the defense counsel or revealed to the jury, and the prosecution still denies a deal was ever made. However, Weiner's sentence was drastically reduced after the trial ended and he was later released after serving only thirty-nine months of his 120-month sentence.

Gilliam was a paid police drug informant and repeat offender, with past arrests ranging from robbery to attempted murder. On April 12, 1995, the same day as the Monfils arrests, Gilliam was arrested for allegedly using a butcher knife to threaten his girlfriend. He shared a jail cell with Rey Moore. At the Monfils trial,

Gilliam testified that while sharing a cell with Moore, Moore had confided in him (Gilliam) about how he (Moore) and Kutska had participated in the beating. In 2000, Gilliam was arrested for first-degree intentional homicide, for the murder of his wife. He's currently serving a life sentence and is ineligible for parole.

The jury from the city of Racine, Wisconsin, was sequestered for the entire twenty-eight-day trial. It was hard for them to keep the defendants straight. Some were reportedly seen catnapping during the trial. After eight hours of deliberation for all six men, they came back with six guilty verdicts, and ninety minutes after that, they were on a bus heading back home.

As John disclosed a litany of disturbing facts about the case, familiar images formed in my mind. It became clear to me that these six men and their families had been subjected to bullying. They were looked upon with disgust by people in the community who believed in biased local news sources. From the start, authorities alleged the men were the perpetrators despite information they received confirming their innocence and despite the fact that the men continued to cooperate with the police throughout the entire investigation. These men did not receive their own individual trials because the state argued this would cost taxpayers too much money and incur additional emotional trauma on to the Monfils family. This prejudicial disadvantage was a devastating blow to the men and their families when the trial ended with six guilty verdicts. To the rest of us who believe as they once did, that the intent of our justice system is to make sure only the guilty are convicted, this case represents a glaring wake-up call. In that context, a saying by the late Sir William Blackstone weighs heavily: "It is better that ten guilty persons escape, than one innocent suffer."

My anger surfaced time and again as John continued to weave this bitter tale. Finally, I blurted out my contempt. "You have got to be joking," I said. "This sounds ludicrous." John agreed and, in a docile manner, sat on the edge of the couch avoiding my stare. "Where is the outrage over this obvious injustice?" I pressed. "Why is nothing being done about it?"

John managed a smile. "Your reaction is quite refreshing," he said, saluting my indignation. "Maybe there's a possibility that you can get involved with our mission to free the other five men."

I surmised John's calmness stemmed from being entrenched in this circumstance from its inception. I was only learning about this sordid tale for the first time. Well into his narrative, he opened up about his true motives for sponsoring this project. "I was married to Mike Piaskowski's sister, Francine, for many years," he said. "During that time I got to know Mike very well. But then Francine and I got divorced. And 'Pie,' as we call him, is the kind of person who says that once you are family you're always family, no matter what." John's voice cracked as he further stated, "Mike Pie is the finest man I've ever known. I always knew that he did not commit any murder. He would never commit a vile act like that." John said Denis always had it in the back of his mind to do a book about this case, partly because he worked with Pie's father, Fran Piaskowski, years ago at Sears during Denis' college days. Based on his respect for Fran, Denis is quite certain "no son of Fran Piaskowski ever killed anyone."

The details, all of which John contended were factual, were overwhelming. They were more than I could absorb, or stomach for that matter, but I was impressed by John's ability to refine them so we all could grasp at least the surface of what had happened and begin to understand why this case was so flawed. Two bizarre aspects of the case stood out for me: 1) the prosecution's inability to produce physical evidence, any credible eyewitnesses, or a single confession during the two-and-a-half-year investigation and 2) the unfairness of being subjected to a joint trial. "Why didn't these men have separate trials?" I demanded. "Isn't that violating their basic civil rights?"

"You are correct," John said. "I think the authorities realized they could never have convicted all six men if they'd conducted separate trials. What evidence they believed they had was too flimsy to stand alone. And I think trying them together greatly influenced the jury into believing that all of them were guilty beyond a reasonable doubt."

"But how can people be convicted with no evidence or eye-witnesses?" I argued. "This makes no sense."

John's mention of reasonable doubt brought up an inter-esting aspect of this case. The opening statement by the prose-cution was revealing, although the jury did not seem moved by it. By stating there were "gaps"—an admittance of their inability to provide a complete interpretation of the facts in the case—they essentially told the court there was reasonable doubt about the guilt of these men. Reasonable doubt is the standard used in criminal trials. When a defendant is prosecuted, the burden is on the prosecutor to prove the defendant is guilty beyond a reasonable doubt—the highest burden of proof the law imposes on any party in court. If the evidence creates doubt, it is then the duty of the judge and jury to find the defendant not guilty. However, the more I learned about these convictions, the more I realized a suspect is often considered guilty until proven innocent.

Like Clare had said, many of the details of this case didn't add up. What intrigued and mystified me was as children we are taught to trust law enforcement and to find a police officer if we are in trouble because they are the ones who will protect us. As adults, we believe the courts are fair. But this is not always true, and many find this out the hard way, like when they're subjected to a wrongful conviction. John had learned all of this firsthand in the mid-90s when his family was caught up in this tragedy.

As he delved further into this drama, John promoted his belief that the convictions were orchestrated on many levels in the legal community where this happened; from the police department, to the lead detective, to the prosecutor, all the way up the judicial ladder. "The legal community bands together in a small town like ours," he said. He talked about the altered time-line of events regarding the victim's disappearance, and witness statements that had been coerced or doctored to fit the police theory. He discussed the botched crime scene. "They didn't even cordon off the area until much later in the day. Mill workers, and law enforcement alike, trampled the area like a herd of cattle, destroying any potential evidence," John said. "The entire investigation was flawed from day one." It was clear to me, from what John was saying, that these men never had a chance.

John's analysis ate at me for weeks. I was furious. I thought of how it might feel to have a member of my own family unfairly taken from me and treated in this manner. It was unbearable to think this could happen to my husband, my son, to one of my siblings, or to me. I thought of how being wrongly accused of a heinous crime and sent away for something you didn't do had to be one of the worst fates imaginable. I thought of how the circumstances could affect my life, my values, my ability to trust, or cause internal panic because someone I love is now locked up with dangerous criminals. Think of the anger, the hopelessness of having your rights denied, your freedoms, sanctity, and everything you hold dear ripped from you. This is unfathomable, deplorable, and wrong.

Clare lightened the mood somewhat to tell us about her longtime friendship with Reynold Moore, prior to this incident. "Rey and his wife invited me to their house all the time. I didn't have a car back then, so I'd ride over on my bicycle. Rey always threw it into the back of his pickup and drove me home if it got too dark before I left because he was worried about my safety. I know that Rey is not a criminal!" she said.

In 2015, my husband Mike and I visited Rey for the first time. I shared what Clare had said about him. His face lit up as memories of their friendship filled his thoughts. Rey was grateful for her continued support. He remembered seeing her in the courtroom during his last appeal. "I didn't know for sure who she was at the time, but she looked familiar," Rey had told us.

John thought the book would be available for purchase soon. He promised to give me a signed copy. For my birthday he gifted me a hardcover version of the book signed by him, Denis, and Mike Pie.

The book was difficult for me to read, even after having discussed much of it in depth with John. The number of people involved, the mind-numbing facts, and the legal references to John Doe hearings and the lawsuits against the men, the state, and the police department, all presented a challenge for someone like me who knew nothing about our criminal justice system. I had to constantly refer back to previous chapters in order to remember the endless cast of characters and to keep track of who supposedly did what.

As I read further into the book, I'd become so angered by the unfairness of it all, I'd have to put the book down. There were times I'd cringe at the absurdity of things like a "repressed memory" from one key witness who was a proven murderer, another who was a paid informant, and a third who admitted to being coerced. Even two of the original attorneys were sent to prison after the trial for their own offenses, with one of them possibly in the same prison as his former client. Depending on how well the state's case was progressing, the importance of these key witnesses seemed to change with the wind. In my opinion, the police department's release of the cassette tape of Tom Monfils' 911 call was the motivating factor for the department to resist the suicide theory. By the time I finished the book I was emotionally drained. And I, like John, had become personally involved.

I grew up in a large family in a small town in the Upper Peninsula of Michigan. I considered us to be poor. There were many things I was ashamed of, including the outdated and ragged hand-me-down clothes I wore. The dilapidated house we lived in was a blight on the block that begged for repairs and updates. The inside was a hoarder's haven, cluttered with endless piles of junk that had collected over the years. Lining the walls and covering nearly every surface were boxes of discarded clothing my mother was saving to make rag rugs, along with receipts, newspapers, and miscellaneous items she could never let go of. I'd seen how organized and beautiful my friends' homes were and I lived in constant fear they might find out about the mess in which I lived. They'd surely make fun of me and tell other kids about it. I became introverted and withdrawn, pushing away the few friends I had. In the process, I attracted bullies whom I was unable to defend myself against. They took advantage of my reticence and taunted me at every available opportunity with their sarcastic remarks and finger-pointing. I was only asked by classmates to engage in sport-related activities when they found themselves in need of one more player and no one was left to pick. I wanted to scream, to fight back in some way, but I was afraid of getting into trouble for being an antagonist. So, I endured the abuse. No one defended me. I suffered alone. As I read the Monfils book, many of these feelings resurfaced and I relived those old feelings of fear, doubt, isolation, and worthlessness. A life I had been subjected to as a child was what I read between the lines of this story.

The most catastrophic aspect of this case was that until the bitter end, the six men, who were all law-abiding citizens, believed in a legal system that was fair and that would ultimately prove their innocence. Instead, they were victimized, tossed aside like garbage, and taken from their loved ones. I learned about how the lives of their families were turned upside down because of these convictions. I started to refer to the family members of the six men as the "collateral damage" of wrongful convictions because of the enduring emotional scarring, financial woes, and exposure to ongoing contempt from an unsympathetic community that was lied to and unwilling to accept other points of view. The families lost the ability to trust anyone. Even friends turned their backs on them and became distant, readily accepting the lies. Money became a concern when their men—the primary wage earners—were absent and funds from savings accounts were drained. Some families had to sell their homes and combine living arrangements to survive, and they grappled with additional trauma resulting from failed appeals, and adjusting to life without a husband, father, or brother.

Another piece of information John alluded to that weekend came as a total surprise but added a glimmer of hope for the other five men. "Our family got lucky," he said.

In 2001, five and a half years after the men were convicted, a major development occurred. A writ of habeas corpus was filed on Mike Pie's behalf. This is an order to bring someone who has been criminally convicted in state court to a federal court. Senior federal US district Judge Myron Gordon (1918-2009), from the Eastern District of Wisconsin, ruled the evidence against Piaskowski was insufficient to sustain the conviction. In his statement, Gordon noted the only evidence was that Piaskowski reported Monfils missing minutes after Monfils disappeared. He was with five other defendants before and after the alleged beating, but was not cited as having participated in the alleged incident. He was cleared of all charges and released from prison. A total of five federal judges had essentially graded the jury as "unreasonable" and "irrational" and charged it with "failing its duty." In his ruling overturning Pie's conviction, Gordon also stated the case against Pie was based on "conjecture camouflaged as evidence" and that "a guilty verdict required the jury to pile speculation on top of inferences that were drawn from other inferences...such a verdict is not rational."

John talked about the difficulties the jury faced. "When we contacted the jurors in 2007 while writing the book, most of them wouldn't speak to us," he said. "However, one of them did." John repeated a statement made by the juror which was completely outrageous. "It was too much to process and too easy to just make the same decision for [all] of the defendants."

Mike Pie was released on bond on April 3, 2001, while the state appealed Gordon's ruling. On July 10, 2001, the Seventh Circuit Court of Appeals upheld Gordon's decision and added, "The jury's conclusion that Piaskowski participated in the beating and/or conspired with the other defendants to kill Monfils is speculation." The Court of Appeals upheld Gordon's ruling. Mike Pie could never be retried for this crime and the case was dismissed.

"Essentially, Mike Pie was exonerated," John said. "That's the term used by organizations such as the Innocence Project to describe a person being cleared of a conviction based on new evidence or proof of innocence. It was a great day when we learned that news."

"Mike Pie was a big help with details for the book," John explained. "He was able to fill in the blanks that we were not privy to. He was at the mill that day. He knew exactly what happened. He gave us valuable feedback about how the mill was run, and technical aspects of how paper machines operate, etc. He'd also saved all of the documentation he acquired about the case. He had file drawers filled to capacity in his basement. He became our eyes and ears of what happened inside the mill in the days before and after Monfils' disappearance. This project took eight years to complete. It became our labor of love. Mike Pie, Denis, and I put every ounce of energy we had into this book for no other reason than to help the other five men, because unfortunately, Mike Pie is still the only one of the six to be exonerated."

I managed to finish the book by Thanksgiving. By then, Clare had heard plenty from me regarding my outrage and disbelief over this tragedy. My husband Mike and I were planning to spend an extended holiday weekend in Titletown USA (a term used by Green Bay locals to indicate the city's high ranking of overall sport team championships despite its modest population). For me, this place represented a grave injustice. Clare mentioned John and the others had a book signing scheduled in Green Bay that same weekend. "I'll take you over to meet Denis and the exoneree, Mike Pie," she said. "They are great guys, and I think you and Mike should meet them."

3

SIGNING UP FOR A CAUSE

On the Saturday after Thanksgiving, Clare drove Mike and me to The Reader's Loft bookstore in Green Bay. The guys—John, Denis, and Mike Pie—were set up at a table near the entrance. John acknowledged us briefly as we walked into the store. All three were engaged in conversation with patrons who had gathered around them, so Clare and I stood nearby and waited. My husband had wandered off. He was in a bookstore. Enough said.

There appeared to be genuine interest in this story judging from the dialogue we could hear among the crowd. Most people seemed to either know some of the convicted men or the authors. Although sadness was apparent on the many faces, there was also a hopeful energy in the air as if the book's contents might enlighten the public and ultimately help the men in prison.

"This book lays out the absolute facts in this case," I heard Denis say.

"I combed through three laundry baskets full of information to create a more accurate timeline," said John to a customer as she paid for her copy.

Many were there to support the idea behind book sales, which was to raise funds to hire legal counsel for the men still in prison. I learned much later that some in the community had accused the authors of profiting from this tragedy, but I sensed early on that this project was more of a mission for them. Eight years of their lives had produced an astounding compilation of factual details that opened my eyes to a profane side of a flawed case and of our overall judicial system. The dedication they'd poured into producing this book was not about profit margins.

There was plenty of buzz about the publication of this book in the local news. Opinions varied. Some said it depicted a true account of what happened, but one critic stated it was "a complete and utter waste of time." Many felt it contained no new revelations about the case. I was angered by the negative comments. I felt they were ignorant and undermined or lessened the importance of the other victims of this tragedy—the friends and the families of the convicted men. Their story had never been reflected upon, until now. But even as the rhetoric flowed, I was pleased this controversy was surfacing. I hoped it could broaden the attention of the case.

John found a free moment to greet us. "You look respectable in a suit and tie," I said.

He laughed as he apologized for the delay. He took us over to meet Denis, who was also wearing a suit. The contrast between Denis' white hair and bright blue eyes was striking. He towered over Clare and me as we shook hands. "Welcome, Joan. Hello, Clare," he said. He looked at me and said, "John has told me all about you and your spirited opinions of this case. It is indeed a grave cataclysm. I appreciate your interest and for coming today."

My admiration for Denis was immediate. I sensed a voracious compassion within him as we spoke. His tenacity to fix this injustice and his commitment to publicizing it was sincere and contagious. I was encouraged by his outspoken and unyielding nature to send a direct message to the authorities that this controversy was not going away anytime soon. Clare and I stepped aside to allow other people to speak with Denis. As we walked away, Denis said, "Make sure you talk to Mike Pie. He's the one who truly understands the scope of this tragedy."

John introduced me to Mike Pie, the exoneree, a man whose nightmare of living a life behind bars had ended. He was fully exonerated, meaning he had regained the same freedoms as every other American. He is able to vote, buy a firearm, and is legally absolved of being considered a felon. Ever since his release, Mike Pie has resolved to exposing the truth about this case and bringing justice to the other five men.

Clare stood talking to John, which gave me an opportunity to speak with Mike Pie alone. Like John, he gave big bear hugs. "This must run in the family, and will take some getting used to," I thought.

Mike Pie was easy to talk to. His manner of dress, which consisted of jeans and a button-down shirt, matched his relaxed and carefree attitude. "I'm going to live my life how I see fit from now on," he said. His unabashed and unapologetic tone was warranted, given the horrific experience he had endured. But he was friendly and animated as he spoke nonstop, using hand gestures to convey his emotion. I was grateful for his assertive nature, as I struggled to augment a conversation with someone who'd been in prison for a crime he didn't commit.

In this setting, with the emphasis being placed on a book about a devastating and personal tragedy, I was afraid to say something offensive, silly, or ignorant. Do I ask what prison was like? Do I say I'm sorry for his grief? He was open about his experience but I didn't want to insult or embarrass him in any way. So I let him do most of the talking.

Mike Pie made an impactful statement to me right away. "I was fortunate enough to have been freed but the other five men are still in prison, and it's my duty to help them however I can." I was moved by this declaration and the tears that shone in his eyes as he spoke. The honesty regarding his incarceration and the suicidal tendencies many inmates experience from being locked up seemed to be second nature to him, but the realities were frightening and heartbreaking to me.

Mike Pie harbors no malice when he states how he lost everything—his family, home, and a good-paying union job with a pension. He now works for little pay and lives in modest surroundings. As he points these things out, you never get the sense he's complaining. He accepts what happened and that he cannot change the past. He is grateful for his freedom and, as with most exonerees I've since met, he refuses to relive the anger he once felt.

As the crowd dissipated, we gathered to talk about the effect this book could have in the future. I was certain of my interest to get involved, and this book event gave me an idea of how to help. "If you want, I can take books home to try to sell in Minneapolis. It might help to promote your efforts," I said. "But whether I'm any good at selling them is another matter altogether." The guys were thrilled.

As we prepared to leave, John said, "Bring the money for the sold books on your next visit."

"You are trusting and very sure I will succeed," I said.

John chuckled. "You have your sister Clare's determination. Plus, I know where you live."

That evening my mind wandered back to my conversation with Mike Pie. His unruffled attitude and determination left a profound impression on me. His was the defining face of this injustice. The clarity in his words begged for the vindication of the others, and his dignified attitude toward those who had bullied him was astounding. "There's no love lost for those who did this to me but I still see goodness in them," he had said. I admired his ability to forgive, despite the abuse he'd suffered. There was a lot to be learned from this man and from his deeply rooted beliefs that caused me to reevaluate how I felt about those who had hurt me. I felt a definite connection between us.

Being involved in this cause meant standing up to bullies. This was something that unnerved me, but it was a necessary step if I was ever going to get beyond my past. I was grateful for the extraordinary circumstances that had led me to this place in time. Maybe my assistance could make a difference. In spite of the dismal circumstances, the prospect of becoming a part of this movement was exhilarating.

4

EARNING A TITLE

After Thanksgiving, an array of thoughts invaded my mind—continued disbelief toward our criminal justice system, sadness for the victims in this case, and admiration for those who stood in their defense. These thoughts never lessened or dissipated over time, and my determination grew as I tried to reckon with what had happened. The situation was, and still is, repulsive to me.

I experienced self-doubt as I contemplated the box of fifteen books John and Denis had sent home with me. I was unsure about my ability to sell them, about who'd be interested or even have the time to read the 487 pages of highly detailed facts and data. I questioned who'd believe the story, and I couldn't ignore my own conscience asking me, "What did you get yourself into this time?" Reactions from potential buyers about a possible suicide nagged at me. This was a bold hypothesis because there were overbearing arguments in the book, leaning toward an alternative mill worker who may have killed the victim. And people typically avoid the uncomfortable subject of suicide. They like to rationalize it away by saying nobody in their right mind would take his own life in this specific manner. And while this is absolutely true, they neglect to consider anyone with thoughts of suicide is never in a rational state of mind. The fact remained numerous fellow mill workers who worked with and knew Monfils felt he was capable of ending his own life. Their arguments seemed believable.

I also found the title of the book troublesome. John had explained the use of the word conspiracy as a direct play on the prosecution's claims of a "union conspiracy to commit murder." No matter, it conjured images of paranoia, the wearing of tin-foil hats, and of living in remote shacks in the wilderness. I also worried others might dismiss this book as a defamation of our entire judicial system. However, in an age where police brutality and record-breaking numbers of exonerations fill news head-lines, this criticism no longer sounds ludicrous. I eventually dis-missed these concerns and focused on my commitment to civic duty. "This is not up for debate," I thought. "I will sell these books. I will find a way to help out. I said I would, so I shall. I will help to find justice for these men."

My husband Mike offered needed encouragement. "While we were in Green Bay talking to the guys, it sure seemed like a no-brainer," I said to him one day. "But now I'm not so sure I can sell these books."

Mike talked me through my dilemma, as he always does, proving he understands me better than I do myself. He's intui-tive about my moods, and he inspires me to forge ahead despite self-doubt. There was a time when he voiced his concern about my involvement in this mission because of the uphill battle it presented; he understood my tendency to become overly opti-mistic before I evaluate a situation. He also knows how disap-pointed I can be if I fail. But rather than dissuade me, he offered a warning laced with encouragement. "Changing the outcome of this situation may be harder than you think, but I know you'll find a way," he said.

Mike's thirty-year engineering career kicked in and he voiced a plausible solution. "Start small with friends and people at work," he said. "Build up from there." This advice motivated me to sell all fifteen books in a month. I acquired more books, and they sold. Seems I had a knack for engaging people and persuading them with my passion and enthusiasm. I continued to pour sim-ilar energy into every sale and in less than six months I sold over one hundred books. Moral support increased. People were reading the story and they cared. Conversations started at work, at company parties, and with friends. I even overheard my husband praising my efforts at various gatherings, which meant his enthusiasm had grown. He eventually helped out at fundraisers and traveled with me to the prisons to meet the five incarcerated men, all of whom graced him with gratitude for his sponsorship of my mission.

This surge in readership was acknowledged on a trip to John's house to pick up more books. John presented me with a box of business cards complete with my name and title of Midwest Marketing Director. I was delighted and surprised. "This recognition is a bit overstated for selling a few books," I quipped.

"You've earned it, and it's the least we can do since we're not paying you," John said. "Besides, titles are cheap."

5

FAMILY CONNECTIONS

U ntil the spring of 2015 I worked part time as a packing assistant for Gentle Transitions, a Minnesota company founded in 1990 by Mercedes Gunderson—a woman who experienced through her own family, the unique challenges seniors face when moving. Because of her ingenuity, an agency to help make the transition easier was born. My employment lasted close to ten years until my focus centered on this new calling. During my time at Gentle Transitions, my bosses, Bill and Diane, and many coworkers were supportive of my mission. They bought books, made monetary donations, and participated in related events. And sometimes they'd get caught up in unexpected situations.

One of our large jobs required every employee to help with transporting an entire building of clients from an old assisted living facility to a brand-new one. Each individual apartment was small, with one client occupying a space consisting of a single room and small bath. But these were intense moves because of the number of clients we had to work with in a narrow time frame, usually completing the job in two to three days. Each of us was assigned multiple clients and, on this particular day, my list included packing up an apartment occupied by an older gentleman whom I will never forget.

The man's room was filled with a large collection of memorabilia from the NFL's Green Bay Packers. Green-and-gold blankets, jerseys, and various trinkets were on his bed, on the furniture, on shelves, hanging from door handles, and walls. His obsession gave me the impression he had more of a connection with Wisconsin than Minnesota. If that was true, maybe he remembered this case, unless, of course, he had relocated to Minnesota before it happened. He was not in the room that day but Tammy, my move manager, assured me he'd be there the following day.

As predicted, the client was there with his daughter on the second day. I asked the daughter where they were from. "Green Bay," she said.

Her dad heard us talking and began reminiscing about his souvenirs. He then mentioned he had a nephew who worked at a business in Green Bay that produced promotional videos for the Green Bay Packers. I stopped what I was doing and looked up. "Are you talking about Mark Plopper?" I asked.

The client nodded yes. "Do you know him?" he asked.

"I do," I said. "And you must also know who Mike Piaskowski is because they are related through marriage. I met Mark on one of my trips to Green Bay for an event. He likes wearing hats and dark sunglasses and he belongs to a rock band with a cool name, Conscious Pilot. I'm also familiar with his place of employment, called Made Ya Look."

In his response, the client used the same nickname John had used. "Mark is my nephew and he's married to Pie's sister, Christine," he replied. "We visit Pie whenever we go to Green Bay."

"It sure is a small world," I said. They expressed fondness for Mike Pie and gratitude for his release. Trying not to forget my packing duties, I worked furiously as I told them about my connection with Mark, Mike Pie, and the book.

"We heard about the book but we don't have a copy," the daughter said. I shared how I had received mine.

The client left to have lunch with his daughter. I finished up in the old apartment and went over to unpack his belongings in the new space. Nearly every surface was again covered with his treasures, save for one. The only thing missing was a copy of *The Monfils Conspiracy*. I retrieved one from my bag and placed it on the empty table next to the client's favorite chair. The black-and-red cover was a stark contrast to the sea of green and gold.

I thought about the client's delight in finding it and of the hope it represented for the remaining five men.

On another occasion, I arrived at a job site early. As I waited inside for my coworkers to arrive I scanned the list of resident names and apartment numbers. One name caught my eye. My heart raced. The name *Monfils* was listed, and this person's apartment was next to the one we were scheduled to pack up. I wondered if there was a connection to the victim's family. I'd have to mention this to Melissa, my move manager, and see if she'd allow me to ask the client about this. My anticipation grew as I explained the situation to Melissa and my coworkers while we neared the client's apartment.

The client opened her door with a gracious and cheerful smile. "Do come in," she said.

She introduced us to her son, who was there to assist with the move. He mimicked her mood. "Nice to meet all of you," he said. "Thank you for helping my mother."

Before our tasks were assigned, I asked the client if she knew the person next door. "Yes I do," she said. "I believe she is widowed. Why do you ask?"

Everyone there was curious. I promised to explain as soon as I returned. I ran to retrieve a book. Everyone gasped when they saw the same name on the cover. I shared the initial story, and included details such as the involvement of the Wisconsin Innocence Project (WIP), the book being coauthored by a scientist and researcher, and the possible connection between the victim and the client's neighbor.

There were several moments of silence before Melissa spoke up. "I have to buy a book because my daughter just applied for a job at the Innocence Project of Minnesota (IPMN)," she said.

The client's son shared his fascination as well. "I am interested in reading what this scientist has written," he said. "I am also a scientist by trade."

The client chimed in, "Well, I'm curious to know if the woman next door is related," she said. She looked at her son and said, "Let's go!" They ran next door while I stayed behind. By then I was feeling anxious because of my awareness of how adversarial this topic was for the Monfils family in Green Bay. I feared hostility from this woman.

I put the idea out of my mind and began my assigned task. For minutes, the crumpling of paper and the whining of tape holders rippling across box seams was all that could be heard.

Soon, however, the son and his mother raced back into the room. They were excited and out of breath. The son declared, "The neighbor *is* a relative of the victim and she wants to talk to you," he said.

"She's very curious about the book so go and wait for her in the hall and bring one along," said his mother. I looked at Melissa. She gave me the thumbs-up.

There was a table and chair in an alcove near the woman's apartment. I sat down and pushed the book out of sight behind the table's centerpiece. "Let's not rush things," I thought. My body trembled as I waited.

The door to the elderly woman's apartment opened. She approached where I sat, a look of stern bewilderment on her face. "Are you Joan?" she asked.

I stood. "Yes, I am."

"I'm Lillian," she said. She offered her hand. As we shook, I hoped she did not detect my nervousness. "My husband was Tom Monfils' uncle," she said. "But he's deceased now."

"I'm very sorry," I replied.

She went on to explain their situation. "We moved to Minnesota before the incident happened at the mill. There were 'issues' between my husband and the rest of his family, which is why we left Wisconsin. We did not concern ourselves with the events following Tom's death, and I have not been back to Green Bay since my husband died," she said.

I felt sad for her apparent disconnection with the rest of the family and the loneliness she must have felt due to the loss of her husband. This revelation caused me shame. My concern for the five incarcerated men and their families had clouded my concern for the first victims of this tragedy—the Monfils family. Lillian herself was not to blame for how I felt. She showed no anger regarding the case, and harbored no ill will toward me. I could see she was sincere in her interest of the book. Her eagerness to reach beyond boundaries and to understand the opposing side of this tragedy was admirable. It was something I had failed to consider.

"I'd like to read the book," she said. "Do you have a copy I could buy?" I retrieved the one from the table and gave it to her. I insisted she accept it as a gift. "I can pay for it," she said, her tone suggesting I had insulted her. I felt foolish as I apologized once again. She left and returned with a $20 bill.

"My card is inside if you'd like to contact me when you are finished reading it," I said. "I'd be interested in hearing your thoughts." She promised to e-mail me, and I was delighted to receive this brief message soon thereafter in an e-mail:

Date: Fri, 8 Jan 2010

We met when —— was moving out. I have finished The Monfils Conspiracy *and have passed it on to my daughter. There is no doubt these men should be released. Please let me know where it all stands now and what is being accomplished.*

L. Monfils

6

CHANCE MEETING

For an entire year I successfully sold books, although interest remained modest. Friends and coworkers stayed consistent in their support. They'd ask for updates, and they cheered me on when I had doubts about making headway. However, I was troubled by an inability to find anyone with a legal perspective to actually get involved. This was heavy on my mind one afternoon during the summer of 2010, as I walked to the row of mailboxes at the end of our driveway. I grabbed the contents from mine and skimmed through what appeared to be junk mail.

As I headed back toward the house, I heard a vehicle pull up to where I'd been standing. I recognized the sound of the engine. The vehicle belonged to my neighbor, Ken. There was chatter coming from inside the cab so I waved but kept walking. That acknowledgment solicited a boisterous retort from a familiar voice. "Hey Treppa!" I rolled my eyes in amusement. Ken's new friend, Johnny, was with him. I'd met Johnny briefly prior to that day. He reminded me of Colm Meaney, the actor from the *Star Trek* series, with his round face and small, squinty eyes. Johnny did not have an impenetrable personality but he was enigmatic. And he liked to show off his flamboyant side. Both he and Ken started harassing me, albeit in a fun sort of way, so I turned around and shot back a quip or two of my own while approaching the vehicle.

Many of my conversations during the past year had focused on one thing—selling books. Today was no different. After some

31

light banter, I redirected the conversation to focus on my mission. As I talked, a contemplative look appeared on Johnny's face. He sat there listening for some time before he spoke in a serious tone. "You don't know what I did for thirty years, do you?" he asked.

"No," I said. "Why don't you tell me?"

He summarized his vast career in law enforcement, from being a police officer, to heading up security at a racetrack, and conducting high-profile investigations. His career was impressive, if it was to be believed. According to him he knew a lot of famous people in the legal field. Although his narrative sounded a bit embellished, I believed every word. I assumed he might think *I* was the one overstating things, but he indicated otherwise when he shared his rendering of the good cop–bad cop analysis. "I pride myself on being one of the good guys," he said. "But I know there are bad ones out there because I've worked with some."

At that time, I felt a bit uncomfortable and timid about this exchange and his shift to a more serious demeanor. And I felt unequipped to discuss legal matters with this supposed expert. So I backed off from the topic and excused myself, but not before recapturing the playful banter and saying I had better things to do than entertain the likes of them. The truth was I needed to process our conversation. Ken drove his SUV up his driveway. Before I entered my side door, I turned one last time to see him and Johnny disappear toward the back door of Ken's house.

As I resumed my routine, a nagging feeling consumed my thoughts, compelling me to bring a book over to Johnny. I could not dismiss this feeling, so I grabbed one and raced over to Ken's house. I knocked on the door and waited. Johnny appeared. "What can I do for you?" he asked, his tone as genuine as before.

"Because of your background I'd like you to read this," I said. "I want to know what you think."

"How much?" he asked.

"I'm not charging you. Just take it," I replied.

He looked on the back cover then retrieved the money from his wallet. "Here, take this," he said. "Give a book to someone who cannot afford it. I can afford it."

I didn't argue. I took the money and thanked him. "Call me. My card's inside," I said. I hurried down the steps as tears threatened to reveal my gratitude because of what my intuition was now telling me—I had found a partner.

7

A Quest for Answers

Asemicircle driveway winds around the front of our house. Basically, those in vehicles can drive right up to the front door. Large floor-to-ceiling windows make up the entire east wall of the dining room and run parallel to the driveway, making it easy to spot anyone who does pull up. About a week after the encounter with Ken and Johnny, I heard a vehicle pull up the driveway. "Must be the mail truck or a solicitor," I thought. I peeked around the corner from the kitchen doorway. From my vantage point, I saw the back end of a red pickup. I heard a door slam shut and whoever it was, started ringing the doorbell incessantly and banging on the large windows. I looked closer and spied the culprit, but it took a moment to realize it was Johnny. I thought he'd gone mad. His eyes bulged when he spotted me. He motioned furiously for me to open the door. I wondered what was up. Although he was frantic about something, I ascertained it was safe to let him in.

As he entered, Johnny held up the Monfils book. He spoke in a rapid and disgusted tone, "I went through this book three times. I read it the first time. Then I studied it a second time. I went through it for the third time with a fine-tooth comb. Now I want answers!" I was speechless. He continued before I could utter a word. "I've worked more homicide cases than I can count, and there's something very wrong with this one! Where's the evidence the investigator supposedly found? I couldn't find any! And where the hell are the witnesses to the bubbler confrontation?"

he demanded. By then his voice was high pitched and agitated. I thought he might pop one of the veins now visible in his neck. "What the hell is the deal, Treppa?" He drew imaginary diagrams on my wall. "I'm trying to decipher where all of the guys were standing while this tape was being played and where they were supposed to be during the so-called confrontation," he said. "Time is connected to distance which is connected to the probability of these men having time to commit this act! There are too many critical details missing from this book."

My voice sounded weak, given the volume of his tirade, as I did my best to share my limited knowledge of the technical aspects. The layout of the mill, the location of the men, and the restructured timeline were beyond my aptitude. "The authors who wrote the book are better equipped to answer your questions," I said. "I can ask them to drive over if you'd like to discuss the broader details with them. I'm sure they'd be willing to meet with you and give you more definitive answers."

My words seemed to fall on deaf ears as Johnny resumed his outburst. "I need to do some research." he said. "You and I are going to have to investigate. We are going to have to go to Green Bay." And as though the idea had originated with him, he said, "Set up a meeting at your house. I want to meet those authors. Oh, and make sure you invite the guy who was exonerated." Before he raced out, he looked directly at me and said in a deep and authoritative tone, "Set it up soon, and keep me informed of when they are coming. We need to get going on this."

Out the door he went, waving as he sped off. I stood in silence, my mouth agape and head spinning. But excitement also stirred within me as I marveled at what had happened. "Wow," I thought. "Wait till the guys hear about this!"

8

FORMING A FELLOWSHIP

Denis, John, and Mike Pie were thrilled when I told them about Johnny. They bombarded me with questions like, "What did you say this guy does? You met him where? He wants to have a meeting…with us?" As expected, they were eager to meet Johnny. They even adjusted their schedules to drive over for a full weekend.

It felt like forever, but the weekend finally arrived. On Friday morning I was a busy bee in the kitchen. "You're awful chipper this morning," Mike said.

I whisked over and threw my arms around him and laughed, citing an earlier conversation between us. "I know you think I should tone down the excitement, but I can't help it," I said. "I think good things will happen this weekend. I can feel it. Besides, they have to, for the sake of the unfortunate folks in Green Bay. Our mission has been stagnant for the past year. We need a jump start before this fizzles altogether. This meeting with Johnny may be our lucky break."

Deep down I was certain great things were coming our way. This felt like a premonition, a prediction on steroids. I relished those moments because they were rare at that early stage. This connection was too necessary to risk losing. It was something we'd hoped for. Having someone like Johnny in the picture could boost our efforts greatly. And as my dear husband looked out for his overzealous wife, she searched for something greater than her, something greater than life itself, something meaningful to fill an empty void from the past.

Standing in the room where Johnny and I held our first "powwow," as Johnny calls it, I reflected on events of the past year. I'd lost count of how many books we'd sold or given away in desperate attempts to provoke interest. We'd sent books to politicians, lawyers, and many news outlets, like 48 *Hours,* but to no avail. The disappointments surpassed the victories by a wide margin. Now there was a reason to be encouraged.

Johnny was a lot like me. *Go for the gusto* was a mantra we both shared. As I got to know him, I felt an unstoppable force between us. We were effective partners thanks to our complementary talents. Johnny could lead us straight to an interested and able attorney, and I could be the persuasive and inspiring one to seal the deal. After seeing Johnny's reaction the day he first showed up, I could see this injustice had gotten under his skin like it had mine. My hunch told me there was no way on earth he'd be satisfied until he was fully engaged and reinvestigating this case. That's what I was going to help him with. We were going to break this case wide open and expose the corruption, the trickery, and the deceit of the people who had perpetrated this injustice. The crusaders and ordinary citizens, intent on vindicating the innocent, the wrongly accused, and the bullied, would remain under the radar and in the shadows to save the day! And no one would be the wiser, until it was too late...

I was jolted back to reality when the phone rang. The guys would be on the road from Wisconsin soon. The drive from Green Bay to our house in Blaine, Minnesota, took about five hours if you stopped for lunch, so they estimated an arrival time of late afternoon. Before resuming my chores, I allowed myself a few more moments of reflection. "The potential for this alliance is infinite, and there will be no stopping us," I thought. "We will open doors." It all sounded so romantic. How naïve of me to think it could be that easy.

That afternoon, Johnny was the first to arrive. He reiterated his impressions of this case. "Inserting myself into this wrongful conviction stuff is a new avenue for me," he said. "My entire career was focused on making sure the bad guys are locked up. There's irony in the direction I'm heading, but from what I gather, these incarcerated men are not the bad guys. It troubles me that they were convicted with no tangible proof of guilt. I keep asking myself, where's the element of reasonable doubt?" He was resolute. "I am convinced, convinced the authorities not only allowed this to happen, but made it happen," he said. "These men were not given a fair shake when they were deprived of their own separate trials. If details were overlooked, ignored, and even altered, it left the jury to decide the fate of these men with insufficient and perjured information. That is not how our system is supposed to work! As an investigator, I was never personally involved in illegal dealings, but that doesn't mean I was never pressured into doing so."

This last statement was something Johnny alluded to early on. It said volumes about our legal system and why Johnny was so agitated. He knew corruption was not unheard of and he seemed to believe it was rampant in this case. I also suspected he was troubled because he had not been there to stop it from happening. Given Johnny's background, his disdain for how this case had been handled was refreshing and a relief. All this time I had believed the case was rife with corruption, but to have someone with his experience and expertise agree with me affirmed my ability to trust my instincts. I was proud to be bridging this connection between him and the guys and I felt it was reasonable to think Johnny could help us.

Denis, John, and Mike Pie pulled up in John's black SUV. As they piled out, they looked road weary but cheerful. Each time I saw them I was reminded of how this mission wore on them emotionally and physically, but of how they refused to let it suppress their enthusiasm. We all agreed with Denis' tenacious analysis, "Let's see where this takes us."

Johnny introduced himself when they walked in, and his attention soon zeroed in on the hat Mike Pie was wearing, which revealed he had served in the US Army. Johnny is an army veteran too, which gave them plenty to talk about. They soon realized they had served in similar territory in Vietnam. "Assisting veterans is what I do," Johnny had said that day. For a brief time, Johnny assisted my neighbor, Ken, with veteran's concerns. It is why I had run into him at my mailbox and it was why I had the opportunity to ask for his help. There was no mistaking the bond already forming between Johnny and Mike Pie, or the opportunity this instance presented—Johnny's ability to aid this veteran in his personal mission.

The guys grabbed their belongings from the SUV as I set out refreshments. We soon relaxed with small talk and jokes. I rolled my eyes more than once at their banter, and for the first time in years I appreciated having grown up with brothers. I was grateful when the dialogue turned serious.

John reminisced about wading through piles of documentation, police reports, and witness testimony to put together a more accurate timeline. "It is vastly different than the timeline the police formulated," said John. "Theirs is inaccurate and was fabricated to fit their theory of murder. When you look at how much actual time it would take to confront Monfils with the tape, to beat him up, to drag his body off to the vat, dump it in, and then clean themselves up along with the entire bubbler area before going back to work, well, it was simply impossible to have done all of that in the time they said it occurred and without anyone seeing something. Besides, there was no consideration given to the paper break that occurred during that same time frame," he said. "The prosecutor was hell-bent on trickery. He figured that as long as there was reasonable doubt about their innocence, he could convict them. It's a trick many prosecutors use."

There was talk of the investigation, and Mike Pie described his thoughts of the day he was arrested. "They blew it all out of proportion," he said. "They sensationalized it. It was over the top and only for show."

Denis talked about how quickly the jury had rushed to judgment. "Six hours of deliberations hardly seems acceptable to interpret the evidence and then decide the fate of six mill workers," he said.

We were getting hungry. I warmed a meal I'd prepared earlier while Johnny ran home to pick up his wife, Linda. When they

39

returned, Linda's bubbly personality filled the air at the same time Mike arrived home from work. Linda's cheerful presence and robust laughter lightened any mood and, oddly enough, conjured Johnny's sentimental side. So, when we gathered at the dinner table at Johnny's behest, glasses were raised. "I pledge my allegiance to this new partnership with you fine people, and to lend my assistance in any way I can," he said. "The oath I took many years ago is my solemn word to work diligently and effectively alongside you in this quest for justice." He sure could lay it on thick sometimes, but the mood was ripe and given our immediate dilemma, his assurances were readily embraced.

That evening Johnny said, "I want to be clear about one thing. I absolutely loathe those in the legal community who defame their oath of office. It annoys me that persons, whom I will leave unnamed, would crave attention to the point of complete disrespect of their civic duties and to citizens alike. This case represents the worst of any I have ever investigated. Illegally obtaining any conviction is criminal, in and of itself, and it has no place in our judicial system."

That night I lay in bed too excited to sleep, but mindful not to disturb my slumbering husband. It felt good to be promoting something meaningful and important. As I relived the activities of the evening, I thought about each of our guests and their unique perspectives toward this injustice.

In the room next to ours was Mike Pie, an exoneree who had been deemed a murderer and union thug. To me he was a trusted friend who had seen firsthand the horrors of war in Vietnam, only to return home to experience the injustice of being falsely accused and imprisoned. He had every right to be angry because even though he had been exonerated, he was forever tied to these circumstances. During his time in prison his conduct was exemplary. And ever since his release he has remained steadfast, as a kind and forgiving soul intent on correcting an injustice that has upset many lives.

Mike Pie could have looked the other way and left this nightmare far behind, but he chose to devote himself to the cause until the other five men were free. These are not the actions of a criminal. In fact, as a result of being exonerated, Mike Pie can literally say anything he wants about the case. He can claim he did it, without consequence, because he can no longer legally be retried for this crime. However, his only intent is to allow the truth to speak for itself.

In the front bedroom was an author with three books under his belt. Denis' determination and selflessness to promote this one were immeasurable. He involved himself in any and all events as emcee, no matter how busy his life became. This mission coincided and sometimes took precedence over his current activities of teaching journalism, acting as family coordinator at the Oneida Nation High School, and bailing hay for his horses. We'd get an earful about how busy he was, but his belief in the innocence of these men was sufficient to compel him to take on the task of writing the Monfils book, a feat requiring eight years of diligence. His involvement was unwavering and my house became his second home as we collaborated further. "That's my bedroom whenever I stay here, right?" he would ask. "The bed is really comfortable. Helps me sleep like a baby."

Tucked away upstairs was John, a staunch supporter of all six men. But John's love for Mike Pie stretched beyond the unfairness of this cause, and he'd become emotional each time he reiterated the integrity of his former brother-in-law. John's ability to recall and recite intricate details on demand amazed me. "The prosecution said in his opening remarks that if you want adequate details, you're going to be disappointed. Then, in his closing remarks, he said something never addressed during the entire trial when he told the jury that Mike Piaskowski was the one who got the rope and the weight that was used. It's preposterous! You can't introduce something that was not addressed during the trial," said John. "But none of the defense attorneys spoke up because it is considered rude to interrupt during closing arguments." His knowledge was limitless and his enthusiasm contagious. "With Johnny on board, there is nothing we cannot accomplish," he had said. And his charm was ever present. "With you supplying us with such wonderful meals and a cozy setting, how can we fail?" he'd say. He never missed an opportunity to break a solemn mood by reciting some silly joke. But when he needed to be he could be as serious and as sharp as a hawk eyeing its prey.

I observed Johnny closely that evening. He'd pursed his lips and sat there, saying nothing, as details poured out of the three men. I thought it was an inability to find the appropriate words to convey his utter disgust for the nonsense exacted on these innocents, nonsense that he believes should have been circumvented. I knew his thoughts because he shared them on many occasions while exhibiting the same body language—a shrug of his shoulders or sudden shift in his chair. Watching him react to a myriad of malfeasance reminded me of something Ken had warned me against when Johnny and I began to collaborate. "Don't ever lie to Johnny or let him find out that you did, because there will be hell to pay. He hates liars."

Throughout our activities, Johnny was hell-bent on discovering the truths that would bring justice for these men, as well as restoring the kind of integrity he expects within our judicial system. He swore he'd make damned sure the authorities who imprisoned these men would not get away with it. Listening to him gave me the sense he'd succeed.

Saturday morning's aroma of brewed coffee summoned an early riser. John appeared in the kitchen. As I poured coffee, he shared his observations of the previous evening. "That was an invigorating conversation with Johnny," he said. "He sure seems to know what he is talking about. You did good when you found him. He'll be a great asset. He's even fun to be around." Hearing this from John and receiving similar sentiments from Denis and Mike Pie boosted my spirits and self-confidence. I felt I was making a significant impact on this mission.

Thirty-plus years ago, when my husband met me, he met a woman who felt ordinary and insecure. I was on public assistance with a nine-year-old son. I didn't know how to cook or manage money and I was afraid of attempting anything other than menial jobs. I never felt smart, even after earning an associate degree from college. I was a stereotypical small-town girl who grew up poor, voiceless, struggling to matter, and in need of constant affirmation. My husband was the best thing that happened to me and my son. Thanks to his insight regarding my potential and his patience with us, we had become an emotionally strong family. I felt better equipped to take risks, to use my talents to get a good job, manage the household finances, cook scrumptious meals, and to eventually manage a successful small business. But in order to feel truly complete, there was more I needed to accomplish. The Monfils case became a cause that filled the void created by bullying. I was learning to put respect for myself before the fear of what others might think, while putting the concerns of others before my own. Being treated as an equal by these professionals was therapeutic and helped me to escape my own perceived limits.

Johnny and Linda showed up midmorning. Everyone gathered in the dining room with full coffee mugs and high spirits, anticipating our second round of talks. This day was spent talking about what Johnny wanted to investigate further. He brought over a list of one hundred case-related items he felt needed to be addressed.

"There are criteria that must be met in any investigation," Johnny explained. "I see this case as unresolved because of the lack of evidence. I'm all about the evidence, because I'm an investigator. I go to a crime scene and let the evidence speak to me. That is how I determine what occurred—by collecting and then studying the evidence. This idea seems to have been secondary in this case. The authorities were not looking for evidence of what happened. They were looking for anything to pin a murder on these guys, to close the case, and to cover up their mistake of releasing the tape. Having said that, I want to know more about what evidence there is. I want to find out how it was collected? What was it packaged in? Where was it stored? When items are sent to the lab for analysis, they must be packaged in a certain way. But according to what you've told me, there is no evidence reflective of a murder. That is why I'm here. I need to find this out for myself and the only way to do that is to get involved."

Johnny fueled this mission. He became our guiding light. He understood the challenges we were up against, and he was way ahead of us as he went over the list of factors he deemed important. "I've already started an online search for specific documentation related to the case that is accessible to the public," he said. "From there, I need to visit the police department, obtain and read the trial transcripts, interview witnesses at the mill that day, and find out what role the fire department played. This information is invaluable, and is what we will need to give to an attorney once we find one."

During the meeting, we addressed basic strategies to create more awareness in Minneapolis. "This topic is still a sore spot in Green Bay," Denis said. "We need to focus our efforts here in Minneapolis, away from the barrage of rhetoric in Green Bay. The book is our main avenue for spreading the word, so distribution is essential."

"The people I've sold books to so far are very supportive," I said. "We should keep the momentum going." Everyone agreed and we decided to schedule a series of book events in Minneapolis in the near future. "The holiday season is about five months away. Now is the time to plan and grab the attention of early holiday shoppers," I said. "Johnny and I will see what we can do to find appropriate venues."

We parted ways that weekend with a sense of accomplishment. And as Johnny and I worked on possible book events, he privately absorbed infinite details about the case.

9

RALLYING THE TROOPS

The next few months were intense with activity. Based on the numerous trips we took back and forth along Interstate 94 and Highway 29, our cars could've driven themselves to the precise locations. We started referring to Highway 29, the stretch of secondary highway between Interstate 94 and Green Bay, as "Freedom Highway." The title commemorates that stretch of highway as the location of the Stanley Correctional Institution where Dale Basten and Michael Johnson were housed at the time. Since then, both men have been moved to other prisons.

In addition to securing three venues for book signings and arranging a book club event at Mt. Olivet Church in Minneapolis, there was talk among us of an event that would be held in the heart of downtown Green Bay where the trial took place. As I realized the notorious nature of this case and the magnitude of negative perceptions by the locals, it made sense to flood the community with factual information. We needed to generate new interest in Green Bay, and I felt a rally was the way to do that. We also needed to form a strategy of how to conduct ourselves because of the controversy surrounding it. Our intent to convey these convictions as faulty or intentional was not going to bode well with a community steeped in years of rhetoric from law enforcement and the county attorney's office. We considered the possibility our efforts could invoke vocal opposition. My personal attitude was to bring it on. This could invite media coverage, which was the primary intent.

I asked Johnny for guidance. He was all about action. I realized I was, as he put it, "cut from the same cloth." But I was unsure if these actions were too aggressive. He disagreed and said, "Go for it. Let your presence be known but keep things low-key and peaceful. Don't break any laws or give them a reason to arrest you."

I called John Gaie and learned an event similar to this had already been discussed among the family members, but never went any further. "We should do this," I urged. I told John what Johnny had said.

John agreed and said, "Let me talk to the others about it." John was great for gauging the reactions of those involved. He and Denis could influence overall opinion because of their book efforts. I felt I could count on John to be a candid cheerleader. He offered to set up a conference call.

The call included John, Denis, Mike Pie, and Joan Van Houten. Joan is the stepdaughter of Michael Johnson and a staunch defender of his innocence. Unsuccessful in her efforts to enlist anyone to help their family following the convictions left her disheartened. Her family was shunned and dealt with unique struggles. Joan's mother, Kim, is from Korea where she gave birth to Joan. The language barrier Kim experienced back then made it difficult to understand what was happening to her husband. His conviction also forced her to seek employment and she became the sole breadwinner of the family. And as with the other families, the circumstances caused deep emotional anguish.

John said of Joan, "She's a great resource for ideas and a good representative of the families." I hoped her involvement in this event could help her to heal and summon support from the other families.

Excluding John Gaie, this was my first encounter with a family member. I was nervous and fearful that my assertiveness might be overbearing or come across as thoughtless. But Joan was like-minded. She was, and is, outspoken but respectful. Her anger emerges, but is not directed toward us. "It's time to stop talking," Joan had said. "I'm tired of doing nothing when we have nothing to lose. We've already lost so much and too many years since our men were sent to prison." She expressed deep gratitude for all we had done and she was ready to take this leap with us. I deeply admired this woman.

"Let's challenge the apathy in this community," I said.

Joan predicted a moderate crowd at best. "This situation is still very painful and very real for us," she explained. "As much as we want justice, this will be a hard first step for many but it's one I'm willing to take."

I stressed the urgency to act quickly and to hold the rally on October 28, 2010 at the Brown County Courthouse. This was the exact date and place of the 1995 trial when the six guilty verdicts were handed down. "Let's not wait another whole year," I said. "The time is now." The end of our discussion brought a unanimous vote to commence our first "Walk for Truth and Justice."

Joan's inclination to vindicate her stepfather and expedite his return home influenced her decision to promote this event. It motivated her to form a select group in Green Bay known as Family and Friends of Six Innocent Men (FAF). The group met regularly, to plan the rally and discuss ways to fundraise. It was a good way for them to stay connected. This group defined whether events succeeded or failed because of how it encouraged involvement.

10

UNEXPECTED RECOGNITION

In late summer of 2010, I was on my way to Green Bay to attend a meeting at John's house to plan the rally. While driving, my thoughts focused on the latest efforts, or lack thereof, as they often did while traveling on Freedom Highway. I wondered what the future held for this mission in lieu of our shortcomings. Aside from book signings, book sales, and spreading the word, the bottom line was that no legal help was forthcoming. I felt desperate. Johnny was on edge from getting the same response over and over from every attorney he encountered—that it was much too difficult and too costly to overturn one conviction, let alone five.

When I joined this fight I was naïve about many things, including the attitudes of the residents of Green Bay. I saw a flawed case. I was outraged. I assumed they would too. Fifteen years had passed but the same level of apathy persisted. Nothing had changed despite the authors' efforts to shift public opinion. The loudest critics were hateful and uninterested in considering the facts presented in the book. It was hurtful to hear them poke fun at our efforts and dismiss us as lunatics. I struggled with my faith in humanity and the ability to convince them they had been misguided.

During these upsets Clare kept my spirits up. "Joan, you are making a difference by giving the families hope." But I didn't feel it. It felt more like providing a platform for the pessimists. It was hard to swallow the flood of negative comments. I feared what this additional turmoil might do to these humiliated families.

I knew I could handle the pressure, but what about them? I imagined how it made their blood boil to hear insults aimed at their men. Comments like "rot in hell" or "they are exactly where they belong" were rampant in response to news stories. Labels such as "con artist," "liberal fanatic," and "wacko" were eventually aimed at me. I was told to stay home and mind my own business. I felt like I had traveled back in time to my old grade school, only this was more mean-spirited. The ignorance angered me, but this time it wasn't going to get the best of me. What they thought of me was their business, and I was not about to back into a corner somewhere and tremble. Instead, my determination allowed me to push back even harder in a constructive way to defend those who mattered. The bullies would get no satisfaction from belittling me.

The influx of opinion regurgitated at every turn and was fueled by reactions from those within the Brown County District Attorney's office, who cited the book as complete fiction. Law enforcement officials collectively adhered to the same notion, confirming John's evaluation of the bond within the legal community. I was appalled at the constant, misleading, and untrue misconceptions that still fed a vengeful community. My aim was to send a new message from the families. It was their turn and I'd make sure they were heard. This rally was the perfect platform to stand with them, to be firm and vocal about my position. I would show this town that these victims were not alone and that their side of the story had merit. It was one thing to dismiss the opinions of the families. Of course they'd plead the innocence of their loved ones. But it was another matter altogether to have someone completely unrelated to them or the situation who staunchly supported them.

After arriving at Clare's house and sharing my rant, she cheered me on. I then drove over to John's with resolve to make this rally count. He greeted me in the usual manner with that big grin of his and a glass of wine. For some reason he was in an especially cheerful mood. He excused himself with a wink and went into his office. He returned with a sheet of paper, and as he handed it to me he said, "Have you seen this? Denis just wrote it about an amazing woman that we are affiliated with." I wondered whom he was talking about until I started to read…

Date: Tue, 20 July 2010

One Woman's Story—Can You Help as She Has?

Written by Denis Gullickson

Thanks to the response of a number of you to last week's information release, we wanted to bring you the story of Joan Treppa who was referenced in a couple of places in that release. Joan is an example to all of us of the kind of power one impassioned person can make on behalf of a cause—in this case, the cause of justice and freedom for five innocent men who remain incarcerated in Wisconsin prisons…

The letter listed accomplishments I had sponsored. More importantly, it confirmed Clare's assertions about the concerns of these troubled family members. They were not worried about the opinions of the general public or immediate solutions. They now felt empowered and significant. This piece conveyed it was partly due to my efforts. I was speechless and unsure of how to react because of how far we were from resolving this fight. But I was, at that moment, struck by the generosity and hope radiating from this thoughtful message. What mattered from then on was the firm belief of all of us about the prevalence of true justice.

While writing this book a good friend, Jennifer Thompson, shared an equally affirming statement her father made right before he died. He said, "Jennifer, the last thing to go is hope." To me, this speaks to the immeasurable resilience I've witnessed in these Wisconsin folks.

11

VALUABLE INSIGHT

Johnny and I managed to set up three book signings that looked promising. The first one was held on August 21, 2010, at a large and well-patronized shopping mall in Roseville, Minnesota, called Rosedale Mall. We were given a decent spot, and mall management supplied tables, chairs, and the manpower to set them up. All we had to do was show up and inspire. The event was listed on the mall website and beforehand we had passed out 4x6" announcement cards in nearby coffee shops, bookstores, and other public places. We were sure of this event's success.

John, Denis, and Mike Pie attended. Mike and Linda sat among a modest audience made up of our closest friends and family members. To outsiders it looked like we had a decent turnout. The mall was bustling with shoppers but there was one problem—we forgot to order a sound system.

The place was loud and the acoustics were terrible. When I made the introductions my voice didn't carry well. No one beyond our general area could hear me. The guys prompted me to continue. Shoppers passed by in large numbers, but they kept walking with hardly a glance in our direction. If they did look, it was more out of curiosity than genuine interest. I saw empathy on the faces of those who sat there, watching. I felt embarrassment. This was excruciating.

Nevertheless, those in attendance heard an animated and amplified intensity from the guys as they spoke. No matter the circumstance, the guys gave all they had. They were skilled and well versed with stating their case for innocence on behalf of the five men still behind bars. Their enthusiasm for telling this important story did not waver, even in front of this meager audience. To them, each platform available to us was vital. Their passion flowed into the crowd like a tidal wave as their voices competed with the noise. This is what they did, and it was extraordinary to witness.

This heart-wrenching presentation should have compelled passersby to stop dead in their tracks. Two of them did, but that did not keep me from feeling discouraged, disheartened, and angry about being largely ignored. I had the opportunity to give a speech of my own, but I could not muster the courage during this humiliating experience. The guys later explained their philosophies toward these so-called failures. "This is a small glitch in the overall scheme of things, and an opportunity to improve on technique and delivery," said Denis "But next time," he added, "let's pay closer attention to details, such as remembering to bring the sound system, shall we?"

After the presentation, a schoolteacher approached our table. We had set out books to sell. She looked at the cost and then at John, Denis, and Mike Pie. "I'm very touched by what I heard today," she said. "This is such a tragedy. Thank you for being here. I may be interested in purchasing books for a class I'm teaching, but I'm not sure I can afford them. I'll have to check my budget allowance and contact you later." Unfortunately, she never purchased books.

Another person had also spoken with the guys. "I'm dismayed about what you told us, and I feel bad for the people whose lives were destroyed," he said. "I didn't know something like this could happen. I'd like to buy a book and keep up with your progress." As he walked away he said, "I'll be sure to share this with my friends."

Both of these individuals had come, stayed for a while, and walked away with a new perspective, as did I that day. Theirs was in reference to a tragedy. Mine was another lesson in humility—the fact that others may not care about things dear to our hearts, even when we believe they should. It only takes one or two indi-viduals to make something happen and we will never know the extent of the impact our presentation had on either of them. But after thinking about the event and my specific role, how did I not see this? Both of them had exhibited empathy and in hind-sight were representative of a growing number of supporters we encountered over time. This experience caused me to realize how valuable each event is, and that awareness is a culmination of many events and experiences. Even when only one book sells, knowledge can still travel far as it may have done in that crowded mall on a busy Saturday afternoon.

12

PEN PALS

A year into this mission I started to write to the men in prison. Johnny and I both felt it was time to introduce ourselves. They'd most likely heard about us, but we felt compelled to contact them directly. It was December, so the obvious way to break the ice was to send a Christmas card to each one. This sounded practical enough, until I found myself standing in the card shop trying to decide on an appropriate greeting. Exactly how does one send holiday wishes to someone in prison for a crime they did not commit? How are they supposed to have a Merry Christmas? What if our festive cards come across as unsympathetic or callous? Nothing about this journey was ever easy. I eventually decided on cards with sufficient inscriptions, and I included handwritten notes explaining who we were along with our objectives.

I clarified our mission to aid in their eventual release. I wrote about not being so easily explained away like family members with vested interests, and I closed with a precarious statement—a promise to stay involved for however long it took. I added a disclaimer about possible failure, but countered it with lots of enthusiasm. As I put pen to paper, thoughts of how we might accomplish this miracle eluded me, but it seemed counterproductive and premature to share such thoughts at this early stage. The overall message was simple and positive—we're here, we care, and we will not abandon you. In the weeks following, reply letters arrived. I was apprehensive about what they might say.

Not knowing what to expect, I anticipated negative rants and cynicism. This was not what I found.

The first response came from Dale Basten. He sent a card that read *Thinking of You*. His brief written message revealed gratitude for my thoughtfulness, but indirectly contained a mountain of loneliness. He said, "Thank you ma'am for the mail. It's the right time of year to get it." Dale had taped an old photo of himself to the inside of the card. The caption explained it was taken shortly after he started working at the mill in 1961. It was the face of a handsome young man. I recalled reading about Dale's family life in the Monfils book. When he was convicted, Dale was a proud husband and family man with a devoted wife and two young daughters. This photo represented a dreadful reminder of a happier time before the troubles started, valuable time wasting away with him behind bars, and an ideal existence shattered into a million pieces. Future letters from Dale were full of kind aspirations for longevity and a place for me in heaven. Dale's letter was the first of many to come.

Letters arrived from all the men with similar messages. Johnny, Mike, and I absorbed information about them and about prison life. The letters were powerful testaments to an injustice that caused sorrow, pain, and the loneliness of being separated from loved ones. Many letters traveled back and forth between us. For the men, they became sounding boards to share their deepest thoughts, a link to the outside world, and a newsletter of sorts about ongoing activities. Even when little was happening, or when I felt depressed, writing to them became my way of staying focused and positive. I filled the pages with encouragement, asking them to never give up or succumb to the belief that nothing could change. Many times, those words benefitted me as well because as inadequate as my messages may have sounded to me, the men expressed how reassuring they were. The letters conveyed a renewed belief in themselves, in humanity, and in the concept of eventual freedom. It was a relief to me when I could write about legal activities which had finally started, giving real substance to my optimism.

As our correspondence continued, my emotional connection to the men increased. They slowly became family. My life became less about me and more about their struggles. The things I had faced in life seemed insignificant compared to what they dealt with. I couldn't imagine being separated from everything I loved and having been punished by society for something I didn't do. The isolation they experienced was always on my mind and I started to make comparisons about my life and theirs. Enjoying picnics, parties, dining out, or seeing a movie were things I took for granted, but were things they could only dream about. I could choose to spend time with family during holidays, weddings, or funerals, but they couldn't. Helping a loved one get through an illness, or a pregnancy, or even a simple homework assignment were things they missed. I had a good life. They were absent and isolated, and privileges were minimal or a thing of the past. I was guilt-ridden about their inability to experience the freedoms I had. So I held on to the one thing that would serve as our direct connection and would keep me focused on my commitment to them—the anguish of being bullied.

I sent blog posts I had started to write along with photos of our events—anything permitting them to visualize the outside world so foreign to them now. More recent letters to them are filled with a flurry of activities and the vast amount of interest that has been generated through our efforts. I've done my best to see my entire existence through their eyes, and I've gained an appreciation of what they've suffered. In a mere moment in time their lives were altered, and for some reason it had happened to them instead of me. Still, they are forever grateful that their existence matters and that many strangers care.

13

UNSUNG VICTIMS

About a month prior to our first Walk for Truth and Justice in 2010, Johnny and I followed through with a promise to meet with family members and close friends of the men. I wanted an understanding of who these people were. I also wanted to know how they felt about publicity that would likely develop because of our event. On our drive over we talked about what their reactions to us might be. "Why would they trust us?" said Johnny. "They don't know us from a hill of beans." I agreed with him, but we were wrong. We could never have foreseen the atmosphere we encountered soon after we arrived.

Denis had set up the meeting in the lunchroom of the Oneida Nation High School, where he works. It's located just off Hwy 172, east of the Green Bay city limits. We arrived early and were met by a handful of people, including John, Mike, and Denis. We carried in a large box and placed it on a side table. Its contents would be revealed later after everyone had arrived. Before long, the room was filled with a considerable amount of people and Johnny and I found ourselves overwhelmed with curious stares and greetings. There was uncensored emotion coming from adult children and grandchildren who struggled with a loved one still in prison, wives who continued to defend their husbands' innocence, and sisters missing their brothers. It was heartbreaking, but comforting to see the camaraderie of goodwill and support among them. Gratitude toward us was evident through affectionate hugs, smiles, handshakes, and tears. Our presence mattered to them. It was humbling to witness a silent minority of those who had experienced more abandonment and betrayal than anyone ever should.

Although they shared a common plight, we learned they refrained from socializing with each other on a regular basis and that many family members were absent that day. We were told some could not bear to be reminded of the struggles they collectively endured, and that the heartache was still too raw. Many felt unresolved anger and avoided the risks of getting their hopes up. Those present saw value in attending, but understood the uphill battle yet to be fought. We offered no guarantees things would change, but we hoped they would see our participation as a reason to believe in possibilities.

We met Joan Van Houten in person. She hugged us both as though we were long-lost friends. With tears in her eyes, she introduced us to her daughter, Tiffany. Tif was sweet and friendly, but I also saw defiance in her eyes. One could assume the young age of twenty-two made it difficult to understand the situation, but not with Tif. She was far from typical and appeared mature beyond her years. She was fully aware of the dismal realities of an unjust system. And she was not alone.

We spoke with Brenda Kutska and her three children, Kelsey, Katie, and Matthew. "Their dad, Clayton, is at work so he couldn't come," she said. Brenda was bubbly and talkative. "This is Matthew. He's the youngest and he was not born yet when the case happened. These are our twin daughters, Kelsey and Katie. They were babies when their grandfather, Keith, was convicted."

The girls were timid and shy and their tears fell easily as Brenda talked about them not knowing their grandfather outside of prison. I recalled the photo in the Monfils book, of Keith holding both of them as babies. Brenda revealed some troubling details. "Clayton and I were twenty-two years old and this should've been the happiest time in our lives. We were newly married and starting our family when the trial was looming before us. Keith's wife received nasty phone calls and letters, and some people wanted to befriend her to find out information about the case. It was very hard," she said.

Everyone we met appreciated our interest. Laughter and tears surfaced again and again as they shared their experiences and misfortunes. Their faces conveyed deep loss and a desperate lack of hope. But they had managed to survive without extreme anger or cynicism. Even though they were overcome with grief, they did their best to live a normal life. They loved, respected, and cherished these men, and it was heartbreaking and shameful that no one had come to their aid before now.

Denis instructed everyone to take a seat. About half the rows were soon occupied. Johnny and I waited as Denis gave a detailed summary of the many activities we had pursued in Minneapolis. All eyes turned to us when it was our turn to speak.

Denis introduced me first. I had never spoken in front of a crowd this size before. I was apprehensive about addressing a roomful of people who'd heard it all. Promises, reassurances, and predictions made by shysters who took every last dime and gave them nothing in return. I felt clumsy as I struggled with my notecards, but I did my best to sound genuine. My focus was on a commitment to find legal help for these distraught souls. "We cannot predict what will happen, but I feel an obligation to at least try," I said. "I'm truly sorry for what has happened to all of you. I had no idea these things happen to such good people. It's not right, nor is it fair, and for those reasons alone we want to help." I talked about the support back in Minneapolis, while pointing to the box we had brought in earlier, which held a multitude of candles Johnny and I had collected from friends for the upcoming Walk. "These candles represent the support in Minneapolis. They will light a new path for us that will get brighter as we move forward," I said. I focused on my reasoning for the Walk and called it a new chapter in this fight for freedom and a reawakening for those who'd like to see us fail. "This is far from over," I said. "This is only the beginning of what we can do to bring this case back into the forefront." I asked for more of their patience that day, and expressed my gratitude for their attendance. And I said a silent prayer that our efforts could produce the results they urgently deserved.

Johnny spoke next. He was more adept at this and he appeared relaxed as he talked about the legal aspects of the case. He was reassuring in his ability to get to the truth and to eventually find legal assistance. "In every case, there's some detail that surfaces that can change the whole direction of an investigation," he said. "I know it's there. It just hasn't come to light yet. But it will."

He also impressed upon them the difficulties involved in pursuing this particular case because of how much time had passed, how poorly it was investigated, and the risk of evidence being mishandled, tampered with, or lost altogether. "There is no DNA that we know of, because no evidence was collected at the crime scene," he said. "That's unfortunate, but it does not mean we will not find something to prove these men are innocent. If it's there to find, I will find it."

The clarity in our speeches turned intense scrutiny among the faces in the crowd to brighter and more tranquil expressions. Reluctance was turning into enthusiasm as they appeared accepting of us and our message. But they still held reservations about the possibilities we presented and of attending this Walk. Then Johnny spoke volumes in his message to them. "It's time for the public to hear you, and to see your pain and anger, and to know the extent of how this tragedy has destroyed your lives," he said. "You are the unsung victims. You have been silenced with no one to support you." Two strangers were now giving them ample reason and renewed courage to once again speak up.

In the time that followed and as Johnny's knowledge of this case increased, so did his cynicism. Often in reference to the Monfils case, the attitude "you can't make this stuff up" became his mantra as well as that of many advocates of the six men. He always says that when we met, I reminded him of the ordinary housewife type, a mother, or a sister. He saw merit in what I was trying to do. He was glad he appeared at the right time and place to help me. The Monfils book captured his investigative curiosity, which prompted him to read the book multiple times. To this day Johnny still shakes his head and asks, "How could this prosecutor convict six innocent people?"

When we went to Green Bay to start a fact-finding operation, what Johnny discovered in several months' time was a defined trail of deceit and trickery used by the Green Bay Police Department and the Brown County DA. His assessment confirmed mine and the others', that there was no physical evidence, no crime scene, no witnesses; only false statements camouflaged as evidence secured through police threats and intimidation.

The fabrication of a perceived truth took a toll on Johnny over time as law enforcement colleagues and friends labeled him a "turncoat" for standing by his well-informed understanding that this case was corrupt. It became a defining moment in his life as he became more aware that the oath of office he stood for had been tarnished by a minority of fellow officers who had taken the same oath.

Johnny and I marveled at the experience on our drive home. We also realized the uphill battle we faced. "It was too easy to make promises to them," I said. "We've got our work cut out for us if we're going to get this done."

Johnny replied, "Don't worry, Joan. We have resources and options. I still have people I can tap into. You and I will get this done."

I reluctantly agreed as I recalled the many rejections Johnny had already received from numerous lawyers. Seeing the pain in the eyes of the young adults at this meeting caused more urgency and a greater sense of obligation. Johnny sounded confident but I could not dismiss a simmering sense of uncertainty about how we were going to pull this off. I felt inadequate and undeserving of their trust, but even more determined than ever to never let them down.

14

UNIFIED VOICES

Friends and Families of 6 Convicted in Paper Mill Worker Tom Monfils' Death Form Truth in Conviction Group–"Conspiracy" Book Bolsters Mission

It started as a book proclaiming the innocence of the men convicted of the 1992 murder of Tom Monfils in a Green Bay paper mill. The book, "The Monfils Conspiracy: The Conviction of Six Innocent Men," helped bring together the friends and families (FAF) of the five men still in prison and the sixth man, Mike Piaskowski, who was freed in 2001 when a federal judge overturned his conviction. Now those friends and families and Piaskowski are hoping their unified voices will help spread the book's message, free the remaining five and perhaps have an even wider impact on the criminal justice system. –Green Bay *Press- Gazette*

This story appeared on the front page of the Green Bay *Press-Gazette* on December 19, 2010. It was the first time the community heard about the formation of FAF–the support group for the five imprisoned men. The idea to formally organize was significant in light of what we had learned at the meeting at the Oneida Nation High School.

The monthly FAF meetings took place in Allouez, Wisconsin, at the home of retired English teacher Shirley DeLorme. When Shirley learned about the Monfils case from her good friend John Gaie, she had a startling revelation. She realized Michael Hirn, one of the six convicted men, had been in her speech class at De Pere Middle School years ago. "He never caused trouble in class and I remember him being an enthusiastic student," she said.

One day Shirley's son shared his experience of having worked with Mike Pie. He proceeded to defend Pie's character by declaring, "Mom, that man is no murderer!" This caused her to voice her suspicions about the outcome of the case and she became an outspoken advocate in favor of the release of all five men. With no obvious idea of how she could help, she offered to host the FAF meetings in her home to provide a safe haven in the highly charged and negative atmosphere of Green Bay. She served sandwiches or homemade sloppy joes and fudge to her guests as they engaged in planning fundraisers, fall rallies, and discussions about the latest developments. It was at Shirley's house, where the meetings still take place, that we organized the first Walk for Truth and Justice.

Johnny was absent on the evening of our first Walk. He was trying to maintain a low profile because of his investigative probing, so I was glad to have Clare there to help calm my anxiety. I was concerned about how this would play out, if enough people were going to show up, or if we might encounter resistance from opposing bystanders. I felt good about having created the renewed interest, but I felt inept at projecting confidence and leadership for this event. My certainty about wanting to help was equal to my uncertainty of how to be inspiring. That night, I was way out of my comfort zone as I was thrust into the limelight. I was used to being the one on the sidelines but now people were looking to me for direction. Never in my wildest dreams did I suspect I'd be a major player in something like this. I was grateful to Denis for taking charge that evening. Denis knew the people in this community, and he understood how to connect with them. Maybe someday I'd become more like him and overcome my fears. For now I was happy to just get through this evening.

We met in the parking lot of St. Willebrord's Church near the courthouse, in downtown Green Bay. Mike Pie and John arrived earlier than Denis who, no doubt, had a list of personal commitments to attend to before making his appearance. We knew and appreciated how Denis thrives on an insanely full schedule, and how truly fortunate we were to have his participation for this event. I scanned the parking lot and saw a modest semblance of supporters. People I hadn't yet met were among a crowd of close to thirty people that evening—a crowd indicative of fifteen years of futility. It struck me that a painful wound was being ripped open, and I felt this group made up the toughest and most courageous of the souls who carried this heavy burden.

I met Kim Johnson for the first time. She is the wife of Michael Johnson, and Joan Van Houten's mother. Kim and Michael are the only couple still legally married. Kim's English language skills are still challenging after all these years and her strong accent is hard to understand until you get used to it. She explained to me why she had not been at the Oneida School meeting. "I don't live in Green Bay and I work odd hours," she said. "But I wanted to be here tonight." I recall the sad, but matter-of-fact tone in her voice when I asked her about living without Mike. "You know, you just go on, and you take care of those still at home. You make the best of the situation," she said. This made me realize that sometimes, giving up the fight can almost come as a relief, or a way to cope in a hopeless situation.

In 2016, I acquired some of the original Green Bay *Press-Gazette* newspapers from 1993-95 containing articles about the ongoing case. I came across one describing Kim and her immediate reaction following the verdicts on October 28, 1995. The Sunday, October 29, edition read, "Mike Johnson's wife, Kim Johnson, nearly had to be carried from the courtroom. She sobbed on the courthouse steps as her daughter, Dawn, held her." This all had happened where we now gathered. It must have felt surreal to all who experienced that fateful day. My words of comfort to Kim felt shallow. What did I know of the horrors she was reliving? Who was I to mess with their lives, or force them to relive this nightmare? I had no knowledge of the courage it took for them to show up. I had pushed for this, but was it a good decision for them? Did they want this? Did they see merit in what I was trying to accomplish? Worse yet, were they just going along with it to appease me? "This had better count for something," I thought, "because I see no alternative." I had to believe this rally was the beginning of exposing the truth about this appalling injustice.

Byron Lichstein of the Wisconsin Innocence Project drove up from Madison to participate. Denis invited him because of his current involvement in the case. Byron was representing Rey Moore in a post-conviction hearing involving James Gilliam, the jailhouse snitch who testified against Rey at the original trial but then recanted in an interview with John and Denis and lawyers from the WIP. This was a last-ditch effort to help Rey.

I'd heard good things about Byron, that he was honest, caring, and a fighter for justice. When he arrived, I introduced myself. Byron was approachable and friendly. His smile was cheerful and welcoming, and his words flattered when he told me, "I've heard about you." In his speech that evening, one phrase of his spoke volumes. "Persistence and determination will be the deciding factor to move this case forward," he said. He was optimistic and encouraging even though he knew all too well the obstacles faced when dealing with the Monfils case. His words provided great comfort and have stayed in the forefront of everything I do.

Denis eloquently addressed the crowd, which included reporters from all four major news stations in Green Bay. He led with a compassionate and uplifting speech. "We're here tonight to commemorate six innocent men, five of whom remain behind bars," he began. "But just as Michael Piaskowski was released, we will continue to fight for the release of the other five men as well. There has been a groundswell of activity occurring within this community and in Minneapolis following the publication of the book, and we are optimistic about future possibilities."

Denis asked Mike Pie and me to also say a few words. I kept my message simple, reiterating my belief in the innocence of all the men, of my commitment to stay involved in this mission, and to never give up or accept defeat no matter what.

Mike Pie again hammered home his unwavering stance. "Whatever happened to Tom, happened somewhere else, at the hands of someone else, in some other way," he said. "What they said happened, did not." Behind the microphone our voices echoed off the courthouse steps, throughout the courtyard, and on to the stone walls of the building behind us which, ironically, resembled the material embodying the hearts of bureaucrats who still conducted business there.

Denis then initiated the march around the block. We held homemade cardboard signs that read, "Six Innocent Men," the names of each of the wrongfully convicted men, and suggestive phrases like, "The authorities got it wrong!" In our hands, we cradled the now-lit donated candles fed through the bottoms of paper cups designed to catch the hot wax and shield delicate flames from wind gusts. The media followed alongside us as we left the courtyard and headed north. We walked past the DA's office and stopped, chanting the names of all five men and proclaiming, "Not guilty!" We continued around the corner to the church entrance where we paused to place seven candles displaying photos of the five incarcerated men, Mike Pie, and Tom Monfils. At that exact moment, the steeple bells chimed six times. We stared at each other in awe of the implication that this event was sanctioned by unforeseen forces.

As the candles flickered, Denis recited a prayer. Afterward, we fell silent. This moment was emotional—a shared bond to comfort heavy hearts and to affirm our commitment to truth and justice. We then marched on. Around the corner was our final stop in front of the police department. We again paused to deliver our loudest chant. It felt good to shout, to unload this burden, to scold. We poured all we had into a final shout-out before turning the last corner and walking back to the courthouse. This event was peaceful, powerful, and perfect. The media witnessed deep emotion from anguished families and close supporters of these men who were never afforded adequate opportunity to convey their hardships in the past. Theirs were the stories that led on the evening's newscasts.

Byron, Mike Pie, Denis, and Joan were interviewed. Denis encouraged the media to get a statement from me, but I declined. This moment belonged to the family members. They needed to be heard, to have their say, and to have their pleas acknowledged by this community. They demanded the authorities own up to what they had done. Their message was long overdue.

Joan was courageous. She didn't shy away from the cameras. She stood firm, voicing an unrelenting and unapologetic appeal. "We will continue to fight for our men until we have no fight left in us," she said as tears flowed, exposing raw emotion.

Mike Pie further stated, "By jailing the wrong people justice was not served for our families, nor for the family of Tom Monfils."

Denis made his own provocative statement. "This grave injustice still hangs over the entire community like a dark cloud," he said. "Make no mistake—we will not rest until every last one of these men is released."

Byron spoke of the need to "acknowledge the system makes mistakes, and then work to correct those mistakes." Our intention to correct this injustice was made clear to a community long torn apart by controversy and opposing viewpoints.

The group disbanded after the walk, but many of us gathered at a nearby restaurant to relive it. This event established our deep connection. I felt closer to them than ever before. My commitment to stay involved became even more resolute and my fear of upsetting their lives dissipated. This rally had stayed positive, and we'd sent an important message of hope borne out of tribulation. We'd told the community that this travesty was not forgotten and how proud we were to stand firm for six innocent men.

We were pleased to see the story lead on each of the Green Bay news channels later that night. It also headlined on most stations the following morning. Voices silenced for too many years were broadcast loud and clear over the airwaves. Unfortunately, accompanying them were less savory opinions by the authorities themselves, who continued to defend their actions. Many naysayers masking themselves online and behind social media pseudonyms also spewed hateful and uninformed rhetoric, mimicking attitudes from long ago by those who were interested in hearing only one side of this story. Nonetheless, this event signaled to those within the legal community who continued to back these convictions that this long-forgotten case was shifting toward a rebirth.

Although there is plenty of behind-the-scenes support for these events, future Walks have never strengthened in numbers. If sixty people attend, we consider it a success. Nevertheless, the courthouse steps that once symbolized unmeasurable pain and sorrow now signify positive memories for the families victimized by this tragedy. And thanks to inspiring leaders and exonerees, this place is now our platform of public defiance where all are free to speak out, to publicize announcements, and broadcast new developments. In 2012, we unveiled the interest of a major law firm in Minneapolis. In 2014 the first in a series of legal motions was publicized. Hopeful letters from the men have been read here and generous donations from people in the Minneapolis area have been delivered to the FAF group. Lastly, this event serves as an annual reminder for a community more inclined to dismiss the realities of this grave injustice.

After each of these events I think about how fate brought me to this place and time, and how everything I've experienced has allowed me to accept this mission. Having a larger purpose has helped me to overcome many of my deficiencies and imperfections by accepting them and moving on to more pressing concerns. Taking a stand and believing in something teaches us people will either love us or hate us. In fact, we learn it's those who find it easiest to ignore truth and fairness who display the most contempt. But believing in one's self and dismissing those who try to tear us down only empowers us to find the strength to withstand adversity.

15

TESTIMONIALS AND VISIONS

I've heard it said the heart knows truth before the brain. My heart kept telling me the best thing I could do was to continue promoting John and Denis' book. This path ultimately led to an opportunity at a large congregational church in Minneapolis called Mount Olivet Lutheran Church. Mount Olivet is recognized for numerous community-based outreach programs including elder care, a children's camp, and counseling services. Its parishioners also participate in a monthly book club. Being asked to appear at a book club event at this church was appealing to us because it guaranteed readership, unlike events we had tried in the past.

This event was set up through Melissa, one of the move managers at Gentle Transitions. After reading *The Monfils Conspiracy*, she offered to approach her book club at the church. "I think the club members would be interested in reading this book," she said.

"If you can convince them to add this to their list of books, I am certain I can persuade the authors and the exoneree, Mike Pie, to show up for a later discussion," I said.

Melissa confirmed the book's approval. "I asked Michele, the church librarian, to contact you and work out the details for the discussion meeting," she said. A date was set, books were purchased, and the authors, Mike Pie and Joan Van Houten, made plans to attend.

The drive for those coming from Green Bay on the day of the event via Freedom Highway was taking longer than expected due to rush-hour traffic. But I was too energized to care if they were a little late because Joan was coming this time. By then, she was president of the FAF group and was eager to represent the members during this trip. I was excited for Joan and I had a feeling she'd do well in this setting. I respected how she never minced words when speaking about her stepfather's conviction and how effective she was at reaching those who listened. In her delivery there was unmistakable sincerity and deep emotion conveyed through her words. "The more you know about this case and what was done, allowed, and accepted by the authorities, the more frightening the reality becomes," she'd later say to the audience at the book club meeting. "There were many gross and intentional lies coming from the authorities…and nobody stopped them." What fell on deaf ears in Green Bay became widely embraced in Minneapolis.

Seven of us entered a small room at the church. Johnny's wife, Linda, joined the audience. Michele directed the rest of us to sit in the semicircle of chairs provided. I studied a gathering of about twenty people, mostly women. They were scattered throughout the seating area as they focused their attention on us. This many participants came as a pleasant surprise. They waited patiently as Michele addressed them. "Let's give our guests a warm welcome, shall we?" They clapped, creating a hospitable atmosphere.

A few of my coworkers were there also. Candee was not a member of the church, but she had read the book and was one of my most enthusiastic supporters. Barb was a church member who supported this cause as well. I didn't see Melissa but learned afterward she had a conflict that evening. I felt bad for her because of her role in making this event possible.

Public speaking was frightening, even among friends, and I felt nervous despite the warm reception. Embracing this aspect of my advocacy was always a challenge, but as a way to calm me down, Denis would say, "These small events give us a chance to practice."

I went down the row and introduced each person. Then Denis took over. He gave a brief synopsis of the case and addressed the crowd. "Since you all read the book, rather than us providing additional details, why don't you ask questions and lead the direction of our discussion?"

Mike Pie was asked a question. "Could you describe the events leading up to the victim's death and explain what your life was like both in prison and since your exoneration?" As Mike Pie spoke, it brought back memories of the day I met him. My initial fear of offending him with my ignorance seemed silly now. He was not the type to discredit, or show disrespect for anyone, no matter the level of understanding about his circumstances. Mike Pie was his usual relaxed and genuine self that evening.

Joan was asked, "How has this affected you as a family member of the accused, and what affect has it had on your entire family?"

Joan became emotional as she talked about the fear and humiliation of having accusatory fingers pointed at her family. "We didn't know how the system worked," she said. "We were thrown into a situation foreign to us. We were law-abiding citizens who knew nothing about what was happening. We trusted our attorneys, the system. Because we knew Big Mike (a nickname Joan used to distinguish her stepfather from her stepbrother, Michael) was innocent, we didn't expect he would get convicted. But it didn't matter how we felt, the overall opinion within our community was that he was guilty."

The time flew by and our session ran well over the usual limit of two hours. It was getting late and Michele moved to end the meeting. Rather than leave, however, the audience gathered around us and expressed dismay at the injustice. There were hugs and handshakes. A woman named Paula was particularly inspired by our presentation. She promised to take action on our behalf. "I'm going to write to *Dateline* and tell them about this case," she said. Michele offered to facilitate an exchange of contact information between all of us.

Mike Pie and Joan received many accolades for their courage and resilience. Joan's face spoke volumes. What I had hoped for was happening. She was allowing herself to trust strangers and embrace their sincere appreciation of what she had faced since the trial. In this setting, she was finding something she had lost long ago—an ability to believe in others' acceptance of her pain.

Back at our house, Joan reiterated her gratitude for this opportunity and for the welcomed reception from the attendees. She expressed a readiness for whatever was next on the agenda and shared something with me that her stepfather had written and sent to her some time ago. It was his testament of a vision he had had and could not dismiss. It is a guiding light for the calling I've been chosen to pursue.

This is the vision in Big Mike's own words:

> I spent approximately eight months in Brown County Jail. While I was in county jail waiting for the jury to return its verdict, is when the Lord gave me this vision. This [was] a very stressful time in my life, having been stripped of everything that was dear to my life. I believe the Lord was comforting me with this vision. The vision was in a time in the future and I did not yet understand it. I believed at the time it was of the Rapture. It was ten years before I correctly understood the vision. It began with me walking amid rubble. As I looked down I wondered why I wasn't being cut or hurt by what I was walking on. The presence that was with me said: "It is because I am guiding your feet." I then looked up and it was a summer day, the grass was green and the sky was blue with puffy white clouds. Before me was a blacktop road with a woman running on it up to a Control Tower screaming and waving her arms in the air. Then I looked up and the clouds were rolled away and Jesus was looking down at me and was smiling. This vision was of the institution I am currently incarcerated in (Stanley Correctional Institution), yet this institution had not yet been built at the time I had this vision. I believe this woman was

running to the authorities with some kind of information, the truth about the Thomas Monfils murder. I was reminded that a woman holds the Scales of Justice in front of the courthouse.

I didn't grasp Joan's intended meaning at first, so I searched her face for answers. "There's no doubt this is a portrayal of you, right?" I asked.

But as she spoke, her insinuation became crystal clear. "Big Mike and I talked about this vision many times," she said. "Both of us always felt the woman in the dream was me because of my self-proclaimed mission to help free him. There was never any question of that. Not until recently. Now, both Big Mike and I firmly believe the woman is not me. We don't think it ever was. We believe you are and always have been that person." At that moment, time stood still. Silently I rationalized this to mean I was chosen to carry the torch until I found the next person to entrust it to. I surmised Johnny was this person and that he and I were now working in sync to carry it to the next one in line.

Shortly after that weekend I received the following e-mail from Michele, sent on behalf of the entire book club:

Sent: Monday, October 18, 2010

Subject: Thank you

Hello Denis, John, Mike, Joan, Johnny, and Joan:

I just wanted to thank all of you again, for coming to talk at our Church Book Club meeting last Wednesday night. We appreciated you taking the time to share your story with all of us and we look forward to hearing that justice has been served and the remaining five men are free.

Listed below is the e-mail address for Paula that Denis and John requested. I spoke with Paula on Sunday and she has already begun writing her letter to Dateline. Also, I noticed that *The Monfils Conspiracy* is not available for checkout at any library in Minnesota, so I have suggested to several book club members that they put in a request at their local library that this book be added to their collection.

Take Care and God Bless.

Thanks again,

Chelle
Michele
Librarian
Mount Olivet Lutheran Church
5025 Knox Ave S
Minneapolis, MN 55419

Letters were written to the television program *Dateline*, but no replies were received. And requests to add *The Monfils Conspiracy* to library inventories went unfulfilled. However, in 2016 we were contacted by a producer at Peacock Productions, an NBC subsidiary, due to the buzz created by the Steven Avery wrongful conviction case from Manitowoc, Wisconsin, a town located just forty-five minutes from Green Bay. Interviews were conducted and the Monfils case was finally going to have national exposure on a show called *Deadline: Crime with Tamron Hall*. The segment aired on Sunday, June 12, 2016.

16

MOTHER NATURE'S PLAN

D enis often wrote and sent out press releases to announce our activities. Here's a portion of one such announcement:

FOR IMMEDIATE RELEASE

Saturday, December 04, 2010–Lakewood, WI

Signature Café in Minneapolis and Anoka's River City Saloon to Host Book Signings:

On Saturday, December 11, Denis Gullickson and John Gaie, co-authors of the book, *The Monfils Conspiracy*, will be at the Signature Café in the Prospect Park neighborhood of Minneapolis. Also present will be exoneree Michael Piaskowski, crime scene expert John Johnson, and citizen advocate Joan Treppa to talk about a true crime story that landed six innocent men in prison.

"Treppa and Johnson of Minneapolis have become actively involved in our efforts," said Gullickson. "This isn't just a Green Bay story," said Treppa. "Wrongful convictions happen everywhere. This story made me wonder about our country's justice system. It will make you wonder, too."

On Sunday, December 12, they will also be signing copies at the River City Saloon in downtown Anoka. Piaskowski is an avid motorcyclist and self-described "Harley guy," making Holly's River City Saloon the perfect spot for him to share his story.

A book and a beer promotion will run throughout the afternoon at each location. "You buy a book, and we buy you a beer. It's pretty simple," said Gullickson.

Circumstances surrounding both events were disastrous, even though we'd scheduled them for the height of the holiday gift-buying season in December of 2010. The weather was not on our side this time, as one of the most impressive and memorable Minnesota snowstorms descended upon the Twin Cities that same weekend. For an entire twenty-four-hour period winds blew sideways and dumped plenty of snow over the region, effectively snowing us in and causing businesses to close.

Prior to this weekend, I'd performed an online search and found the website for the Innocence Project of Minnesota. This was the organization Melissa had mentioned at work. Its mission appeared to be about aiding the wrongfully convicted, which was the essence of what we were trying to do. I had sent an e-mail inviting them to our book signings that weekend, and was surprised to receive a friendly reply from the legal director, Julie Jonas. She thanked me for the invitation and said she'd do her best to attend one of the two events. We, of course, did not meet her then due to the weather.

Saturday morning we were determined to make it to our first event, which took place at the Signature Café. This restaurant was small, seating approximately fifty people, and nestled on a quiet residential street in a suburb of St. Paul called Prospect Park. Owners Nathalie and Tony exhibited kindness and offered their space, along with an array of appetizers and drinks to anyone who attended. Prior to the event, a group of us had gone to their restaurant for lunch. Johnny and I had introduced the owners to John, Denis, Mike Pie, and Joan Van Houten. I remember watching as Nathalie held Joan's hands and with reassuring words, saying she and Tony would help out however they could. On this day, however, Mother Nature had other plans.

Right before we left the house, Nathalie called and advised us against trying to make the drive. "We cannot even get out of our driveway to open up," she said. "We're staying home."

We were disappointed as we watched the blind fury of the storm from the safety of our house. I was relieved we had a well-stocked refrigerator to feed our snowbound friends. We spent the day consoling ourselves over hot coffee and soup.

Denis and John had safely driven from Wisconsin the day before the storm hit, but Mike Pie did not accompany them due to a scheduling conflict. For this reason alone the River City Saloon event was also doomed. A poster I'd created for that event, which featured a photograph of Mike Pie proudly sitting on his Harley motorcycle, promised an appearance by him. The poster had been hanging in the window of the establishment for weeks.

In spite of our low expectations for this second event, we weren't going to back out. We had happened upon the saloon earlier in the year and Holly, the proprietor, expressed considerable interest in our cause. She was generous enough to allow us the use of her place, so we braved the residual effects of the storm. The roads were treacherous from the amount of snow that accumulated overnight, and the conditions left little hope the number of patrons would increase beyond the few already there when we arrived. We didn't sell a single book. In fact, we gave one away because of Johnny's creativity. He stirred a pathetic amount of interest by asking, "Hey, anyone know the population of Green Bay, Wisconsin?"

Someone actually responded by yelling, "120,000!"

"Close enough," said Johnny. It didn't matter if they guessed right or wrong. We were going to give the first person to answer a book either way.

It was a relief to pack up our belongings that day. The bad luck was discouraging, and the hours and resources spent pursuing these events left us exhausted. It was the Rosedale Mall fiasco all over again. In retrospect, it's clear we all stood for a just cause and this was part of the path we'd chosen. Although it still felt like we were working our way through a process driven by chaos, the bottom line was, in spite of our failures, our efforts gave hope to the men and their families.

Time was always of the essence, so the following week we formulated and pursued a new and more direct approach—targeted letter-writing.

17

FISCAL APPEAL

Our new agenda was a strategic letter-writing campaign aimed at key legislators, senators, and state representatives in Wisconsin. Insight from Johnny provided ample fact-based concern about the integrity of this case, and we felt taking our message to Madison, a more progressive area of the state, would garner interest.

One specific letter I wrote was sent to the attorney general of the state of Wisconsin, Mr. J. B. Van Hollen. I expressed my angst about the case, pointed out its most alarming flaws, and suggested an urgent reinvestigation. I also appealed to his fiscal side by addressing the costs of housing a single prisoner per year, and the unnecessary expenditures burdening the state by continuing to incarcerate five innocent people. Based on current data, the annual taxpayer costs range from $31,286 per inmate to $60,000. Given these figures, the cumulative costs incurred from incarcerating these men since 1995 are staggering and the unnecessary incarceration of innocent people across the board simply lends to the increase of state taxes.

In the letter, my stance was clear: "[I]n the long run, it will cost the state dearly by the time this is really over," and, "Be aware that it will most likely take some time before we find the right people to take action, but we are searching diligently, and we will find the one person that will do something."

Within weeks I received this response from Mr. Gregory M. Weber, the assistant attorney general and director of the Criminal Appeals Unit of Wisconsin:

December 17, 2010

Dear Ms. Treppa,

Thank you for your letter to our office regarding the 1992 murder of Thomas Monfils, the subsequent criminal prosecution in Brown County, and the recent publication of a book about these events. I serve as Director of the Wisconsin Department of Justice's Criminal Appeals Unit.

As you know, multiple courts have reviewed the case and confirmed the guilt of all but one of the men originally prosecuted and convicted. One of those men–Reynold Moore–has an appeal pending in the Wisconsin Court of Appeals. If the remaining men believe they have viable legal challenges to their convictions, they remain free to bring those challenges in the appropriate courts.

Sincerely,

Gregory M. Weber
Assistant Attorney General
Director, Criminal Appeals Unit

I was disappointed and annoyed. It was disconcerting to have my efforts so flippantly dismissed. I wrote back to Mr. Weber to express my displeasure. The letter was dignified and written more for my benefit than his. In it, I highlighted the statement from him that infuriated me: "…the guilt of all but one of the men." I reiterated the significance of Mike Pie's exoneration and of my resentment toward his attitude. I resisted revealing my deepest thoughts of how I longed for the day when he and Van Hollen would be forced to witness the eventual freedom granted to these men. I wanted them to experience discomfort as news reports revealed full exonerations for all the men, and I wanted it to happen on their watch. But that wasn't meant to happen.

In January of 2015, Van Hollen was replaced by Brad Schimel, the new attorney general who also refutes any new findings in this case. In a Green Bay *Press-Gazette* news article from May of 2016, Schimel argued the new evidence is "so flimsy and unconvincing that no reasonable jury could have seriously entertained any doubt that he [Monfils] was murdered."

No second response was forthcoming from Weber, who was also replaced in 2015, but I was content to have received his first. My letter had been acknowledged. And because it is in their records, anyone who holds the office knows someone is paying attention. I believe this factor holds significant weight in these troubled times.

In addition to past correspondence sent out to media outlets, newspapers, philanthropists, online organizations, and radio personalities in Wisconsin, we widened our range to include Minnesota. Again we received minimal replies, but none that opened doors. Few had an appetite for this cause, and we found ourselves in limbo once again.

This was yet another low point in our mission. We were discouraged and weary. Book sales diminished and we felt the sting of impending doom…again. I worried about how the families and the men felt. Was each letdown another enormous blow, or did it feel like business as usual to them? Did it lessen their hope? Did it cement a belief their situation was never going to change? Letters from the men said otherwise, but were they losing faith in us, in possible freedom, and in their ability to cope? I was troubled and saddened, and Johnny's verbal frustration about his inability to find a capable attorney didn't help matters. Over two years, Johnny and I spent many hours sulking in my family room where we'd wrack our brains looking for new ideas. We'd sit in silence and stare into our cups of tea, as though we'd find answers there. As luck would have it, we'd soon find another reason to keep going.

18

THE MADISON ATTORNEY

"*This case probably represents the greatest travesty of injustice in Wisconsin history"–Ed Garvey*

Throughout 2010, Johnny and I continued to engage in activities with John, Denis, and Mike Pie. We hoped something would give and that we'd find ourselves in the right place at the right time with someone who could help us. While these thoughts settled in as wishful thinking, one major event surfaced that provided optimism. And we were gifted with an opportunity to meet the event's founder.

Denis had an ongoing rapport with Ed Garvey, a well-known attorney from Madison. In 1986, Ed was the Democratic nominee in Wisconsin for US Senate and in 1998 he was the Democratic nominee for Wisconsin governor. Ed had been in the legal field a long time. He had connections that could further our cause. According to Denis, Garvey was an outspoken supporter of the Monfils defendants. In fact, brochures tucked inside each book are adorned with the above-mentioned quote.

We met with Ed at his office shortly after Johnny joined our group. Denis wanted Ed to meet Johnny and to hear his latest findings. This meeting was also a way for us to brainstorm future actions for our mission.

We entered the modest office building in Madison where Ed had his law practice. As we reached the second floor, we were greeted by a friendly receptionist. "Mr. Garvey is expecting you

and will be with you momentarily," she said. "Please make yourself comfortable in the conference room."

The room was furnished with a large wooden table and chairs
in the center, and a tired old couch up against the wall. Upon
entering, Johnny and I were drawn to a portrait hanging on the
wall. We stared, mesmerized at an almost life-sized image of
Paul Wellstone, the late Minnesota senator who was known as a
progressive Democrat and was often a lone voice that stood firm
against status-quo policies on both sides of the aisle. Wellstone
died in a plane crash alongside his wife, Sheila, and one of their
daughters on October 25, 2002, while campaigning for a second
term as senator. The incident happened eight years prior to the
day we visited Ed's office and, although the painting reignited
memories of these horrific deaths, its presence gave Johnny and
me a good feeling about meeting this attorney.

Ed appeared and greeted us enthusiastically. His white hair
revealed years of experience as a practicing lawyer. He invited
us to gather around the table.

Johnny spoke first. For Ed's benefit, he described his process of confirming aspects of the case covered in the book. "For
my own level of comfort, I did my own mini investigation," said
Johnny. "Joan and I visited the GBPD, I conducted private interviews with witnesses, and I then compiled an entire file on this
case. What I conclude, from the standpoint of a detective, is this
case is full of corruption. I'm convinced it was a community conviction involving the police, the prosecutor, and the news media,
all working in collusion to seal the fate of these men. My biggest
concern is the lack of evidence, and I am dismayed at the absurdity of Mike Pie having been the only one released to date." He
gestured to Mike Pie. "Look at him. He served his time in Vietnam
only to come back and serve time unlawfully in prison. I submit
to you what he experienced in prison equates to being on active
military duty in relation to having post- traumatic stress disorder."

"That's true," said Mike Pie.

For the majority of the meeting I remained quiet. I knew I had
earned the respect of my colleagues, both as an outsider and a
woman, but they were the experts and I was still learning. Besides,

my perspective leaned more toward how this had affected the families after the convictions. However, at some point during the discussion, Ed turned to me and said, "You seem intelligent. Why don't you share how you feel about all this and what compelled you to get involved."

I collected my thoughts and replied, "I was bullied as a child, and this whole situation looks like bullying on a much larger scale. It disgusts me to know others have been treated in a similar manner as I have, and that the bullying continues as innocent men still sit in prison. I share the sense of duty you see here today to get the men out of prison and reunite them with their families. I want to be part of a unified voice for them."

Ed nodded and said, "Thank you. That is quite commendable." He listened for a long time to what everyone had to say. He then scanned the room and said, "Well, what do you want me to do? I can contact some people I know to see if they can help. I cannot promise anything, but I can certainly try. If you'd like, I'll see to it that there's a space reserved for you at the next Fighting Bob Fest."

"That would be great," said John.

"That allows us to put books directly in the hands of public officials," said Denis.

Our meeting ended and we felt good about it even though we knew Ed couldn't help us directly, in a legal sense. He had enough clients to keep him busy, and his age was a factor. He pledged to make phone calls on our behalf, which he started doing even before we left his office. "Keep me informed of any news and stay in touch," he said. "And I'll let you know about Fighting Bob."

As we left his office I had to ask, "What's a Fighting Bob?"

19

A Fighting Chance

This truncated press release announced our first Fighting Bob Fest event and depicts the ongoing enthusiasm we maintained despite endless setbacks:

FOR IMMEDIATE RELEASE:

Lakewood, Wisconsin - September 7, 2010
Authors, Experts, and Activists Will Gather at Fighting Bob Fest

Denis Gullickson and John Gaie, authors of *The Monfils Conspiracy*, will be promoting their book and the innocence of Dale Basten, Mike Hirn, Mike Johnson, Keith Kutska, and Rey Moore at an annual gathering of progressive activists this coming Saturday, September 11, in Baraboo, Wisconsin.

Along with exoneree Mike Piaskowski, Midwest Marketing Director Joan Treppa, and crime scene expert Johnny Johnson, Gullickson and Gaie will be talking to progressives at the Sauk County Fairgrounds. Keynote speakers at the event will include Rev. Jesse Jackson, Tammy Baldwin, Jim Hightower, David Obey, Mike McCabe, and others.

"This will give us an opportunity to take our cause to the progressives from throughout the state and the Midwest," said Gullickson. It also gives us a chance to support Ed Garvey, who has become very involved in our cause."

Garvey, a highly respected Madison attorney and political activist, is the founding force behind Fighting Bob Fest. The Fest is an annual political event that has grown from 1,000 attendees in 2001 to over 8,000 in 2009. In July, Gullickson, Gaie, Piaskowski, Treppa, and Johnson met with Garvey to explore avenues for pushing for new trials or the outright release of the five men who remain incarcerated in Wisconsin prisons. Garvey—who serves as emcee for the event—will be plugging the book and the cause from the stage throughout the day.

"At the very least we intend to hand a book directly to the main keynote speaker, Rev. Jesse Jackson," said Gaie. "Rey Moore was a delegate for him when he ran for president. We've had a pretty successful summer expanding our circle through Ed Garvey. If we can get this person involved, we can take our efforts to the next level."

According to the event's website, Fighting Bob Fest is "an old-fashioned Chautauqua" named in honor of "Wisconsin's most famous hell-raiser, Fighting Bob La Follette. La Follette fought for democracy and economic fairness; he busted trusts, railed against the robber barons' control over the political system, called for open primaries, workers' compensation, and unemployment insurance. He thought people and ideas should rule instead of Big Money."

The potential to participate in this event was a step up from sending letters or mailing books that were most likely shelved or ignored altogether. Having a booth could land books in the hands of politicians and activists alike, and we could potentially forge deep connections with them. Ed's generosity afforded us a significant avenue to rouse support for this cause. Johnny couldn't attend, but the rest of us were there along with my sister Clare, my husband Mike, Denis' wife, Kathy, and their friend, Paul.

I anticipated an encounter with Rev. Jesse Jackson. Clare and I planned to engage him, by sharing an important connection between Jackson and the Monfils case. Clare was the bridge linking the two. In a letter to Clare in 2010, Rey had shared these words about delegating for Rev. Jackson during his 1988 presidential campaign:

> When we were on strike at Nicollet Paper, he [Jackson] came to a rally I organized and spoke at the Brown County Arena. While we were onstage together, he also took my cap and never gave it back. I worked throughout the 8th district to get out the vote for Rev. Jackson. I was with him in Oshkosh onstage with other workers in the campaign. I also helped organize a rally at St. Norbert College. I emceed both this rally and the one at the Brown County Arena. His advanced person stayed in my home. As I said before, I would have been a regular delegate but Paul Tsongas had a person he wanted at the convention so my spot was taken and I became an alternate, but I never stopped working. I am hoping Rev. Jackson will get involved.

Rey had always been kind to Clare, and on that day, she was going to return the favor. She supported and trusted Rey, and she never doubted his innocence. She was being given this opportunity to argue her point on his behalf in front of this political figure.

88

To make sure Jackson understood Rey's current plight, Clare and I formulated a simple plan—to literally stop Jackson dead in his tracks. Clare would explain Rey's dilemma and hopefully tap into Jackson's emotional spirit. All we needed was a small window of opportunity.

We grabbed a bite to eat while waiting for Jackson's arrival. As we finished, Clare yelled, "Joan, come on! There he is! Let's grab the book and get into position!"

I jumped up in time to see three black sedans, in succession, turning the corner and heading toward the parking lot. My hopes soared. We only had to wait a few moments before our subject came into view. He headed our way on foot with Secret Service men surrounding him. We'd have to be assertive, yet nonthreatening.

Fortunately, getting close to him was easier than expected. I stayed back to watch while Clare, having received permission, stepped in front of Jackson. He stopped. She commenced narration of her dialogue while resting the book on Jackson's chest. All eyes were on her as she boldly looked directly into his eyes and spoke, "Rev. Jackson, I have a book for you to read about Reynold Moore, a friend of mine who aided in your 1988 presidential campaign. He was wrongfully convicted of murder many years later and remains behind bars to this day. I am here to ask that you help him in his release. Please take this book and read it. Then you will understand what this is all about. I thank you, sir."

As fast as she'd stepped in front of him, she now backed away and allowed him to grasp what she'd said. He paused and repeated her message. She nodded in affirmation. He then handed the book to the Secret Service man behind him, and commenced walking toward the main stage. The person holding the book leaned toward us and said, "I promise to make sure Rev. Jackson gets this back."

Later that day, after Jackson's speech, Clare and I articulated our hope that this encounter would be a turning point in helping Rey and the others. As I paused to watch the caravan of black sedans pulling out of the fairgrounds, I prayed Rey's chance for release did not exit along with it.

Despite our efforts to contact Rev. Jackson afterward, we never heard back from him or his associates. I still wonder if he thought about us, or took the time to read that book. My reasons for telling this story do not rest on what Jackson did or didn't do, but rather to illustrate the lengths we went to accomplish our mission. Although the day was relatively unsuccessful, we had done our best. We held on to the belief that we'd eventually meet the right people to help us.

20

ENCOUNTERING AN ADVERSARY

Trips to Green Bay during the summer of 2010 put many miles on Johnny's RV and pickup truck. One trip in particular created quite a stir at the GBPD and the courthouse.

While Johnny and I were making inquiries at the police department for documents relating to the Monfils case, we received undivided attention from police officers who began to gather and watch us from a room with large windows behind the reception desk. As Johnny asked for numerous documents from a list he had compiled before our arrival, the clerk became increasingly reluctant to release them. She then excused herself, saying she'd return momentarily.

Soon, a police officer entered the lobby from a glass-enclosed room on the opposite end. We both recognized the officer's face from a police video that documented the recovery of Tom Monfils' body from the vat. In the video, the phrase, "Way to go, Kutska," is heard but is somewhat obscure to the ear. While the guys were writing the book, they had the audio portion adjusted to reveal what was said. Shortly after this statement is heard, a young police officer appears. He's pointing to the top of the pulp vat where a disturbance has been found. His face suggests a look of indignation about who may have done this horrible deed. Standing before us was that same officer.

Fifteen years later, this officer had become a lieutenant. He asked Johnny to join him and escorted Johnny into the room. I could see them, but their conversation remained private. As soon as Johnny exited the room, he motioned for us to leave. We got in the pickup and drove off. "He was cooperative," Johnny said, acting surprised. "He told me I can have access to whatever public records I want. But he was curious about why I was looking into this case. I wanted to leave before divulging too much just yet."

On our visit to the courthouse we met up with a woman unfamiliar with the initial investigation. "Isn't that case over and done with?" she asked.

"Not as far as I'm concerned," said Johnny.

"Well, here's what you asked for." She handed him a paper containing the Oath of Office from the district attorney's office. "I'm not sure what you plan to do with that."

Johnny laughed after we left. "I did that just to get a rise out of them," he said. "Makes 'em wonder what we're up to." But Johnny's true aim was to make a big deal of the importance of this oath.

At the end of the week, Johnny felt certain there was no additional information to obtain above what he'd already received. We talked about heading home the next morning.

My sister Clare suggested we dine that evening at a place called The Fox Harbor Pub and Grill. "It has a great outdoor patio overlooking the Fox River," she said. "It's on South Washington Street in downtown Green Bay, roughly a half mile from the courthouse and police department. A lot of people from both places go there on Friday night to have dinner. We can ask John, Denis, and Mike Pie to join us."

The day was pleasant so we opted to sit on the patio. Johnny wasted no time in checking out his surroundings. He always went into what I call "observe and detect" mode because of his fascination with people's behaviors and an insatiable desire to study them up close. He was quite intrigued with the people living in this area who were, as he said, "...more obsessed with their football team than the fact that their county had wrongfully convicted six innocent men." When Mike Pie and John showed up we placed our orders.

Soon, Clare spotted John Zakowski, the former prosecutor in the Monfils case. He was standing near the bar wearing a suit and tie, talking to a likely colleague who was similarly dressed. We laughed when we also saw Johnny standing next to them in his khaki shorts and polo shirt, acting casual. A huge grin covered his face when he saw we had spotted him. Johnny had, of course, also recognized the familiar face of the DA from the many news clips we reviewed.

Zakowski moved and sat with a group of middle school-aged students at a nearby table. He left the restaurant soon after, but it was enough for Johnny to have encountered him. "Wow, I got to stand next to the man who orchestrated this whole travesty," Johnny said. "What a fitting way to end the week." We then relaxed in the company of good friends before heading home to Minnesota.

21

GAINING MEDIA ATTENTION

There were large periods of time when little progress was made. We'd use that time to recharge our mental batteries while keeping an eye out for inspiration to once again spur us in a new direction. In the meantime, small opportunities popped up here and there.

In 2012, John, Denis, Mike Pie, and I attended a second Fighting Bob Fest in Madison at the Alliant Energy Center. The venue was huge with hordes of people everywhere. We hung a large banner promoting our cause behind our designated table, which caught the attention of many passersby. One notable person who stopped to chat was Gil Halsted, a Wisconsin Public Radio personality. Halsted reported on criminal justice issues, with story shorts airing between longer segments. He expressed interest in doing a spot on the Monfils case, so he interviewed John and Denis and promised to let us know when it aired. We were delighted to hear his piece sometime later, complete with a summary of the case and our latest efforts.

Receiving this kind of exposure was gratifying because of the potential awareness it could bring and because media attention outside of the Green Bay area was as inaccessible as legal help. However, opportunities emerged in 2013 and by 2016 we had started to receive additional media requests. One of them included an over-the-phone interview with Halsted who, this time, asked me to share my personal views about the case. The clip aired on Wisconsin Public Radio in March of 2016.

Most of the people who approached our table expressed interest and dismay as we recited the story. We sold numerous books that day, but in the afternoon the crowds thinned. "Can you handle the table for an hour while we go and listen to Senator Bernie Sanders?" asked Denis.

"I'll be fine," I said.

I strained to hear Sanders' speech when a man walking by caught my attention as he halted abruptly and stood in front of our table. He tilted his head to one side and stared at the banner behind me for many seconds. He then looked at me, and in a distinct British accent, spoke, "What's this all about?" he inquired.

I summarized the case. He then introduced himself. "I'm Bruce Bradley. I'm from the UK, but I'm currently living in Spring Green, Wisconsin. I'm a screenwriter. I work with a local theater company and I'm trying to figure out why am I not aware of this particular story. I absolutely love writing about anything crime related." Bruce's face lit up as he uttered an idea. "I may be interested in writing a screenplay about this case," he said.

"If you come back in about an hour, the authors will be here," I said. "They can fill you in on more intricate details." As though Bradley had suddenly remembered where he was going, he said, "I must go. I'm on my way to meet someone, but I will return later to meet the authors and purchase the book." He then hurried off.

When the others returned, I told them about Bradley. "He said he'd stop back over," I said.

"Sure he will," said Denis.

Glances echoing Denis' assumptions appeared on the faces of both John and Mike Pie. "You guys have no faith," I said. "I'm telling you, this guy will be back. Mark my words."

As the event drew to a close, we began to pack our belongings. I was quiet and feeling quite defeated until Bradley appeared out of the blue, just like before. "Guys, this is Bruce," I said excitedly, and relieved, but opting to enjoy my small victory by interjecting a bit of sarcasm.

The guys picked up on it as they all sent an apologetic look my way. We shared some fun banter with Bradley before he said, "From what Joan has said, I think I'd be interested in working with you on a screenplay about this story. Can you tell me more about it?" The guys shared vast details to an interested screenwriter. Bruce purchased a book and said, "Let me read this and get back to you." We exchanged contact information and made plans to get in touch.

The guys followed up by sending additional information to Bradley and, sometime later, he contacted us to ask if we could meet to discuss his vision for the screenplay.

22

DISCOVERY OF
HIDDEN TRUTHS

Months later John held a meeting at his house. In attendance were Bruce, Mike Pie, Denis, Johnny, and me. Cal
Monfils (the younger brother of Tom Monfils) and Byron Lichstein
(Rey Moore's Innocence Project attorney) were there also, having
expressed the same enthusiasm toward this endeavor as we had.

Johnny met Cal and Bruce for the first time during this
meeting. I had not talked with Cal much before that day, so
I broke the ice by giving him a book my son had written and
illustrated titled *MEGA 99: Adventures of an Appalachian Trail
Thru-Hiker*. "It's a journey of the outdoors, depicting my son's
five-and-a-half-month excursion into the wilderness," I said to Cal.

He was appreciative and accepted the gift in his usual
reserved and quiet manner. Prior to this meeting, I had learned
Cal had reached out to John, Denis, and Mike Pie when he heard
the Monfils book was being published. He was curious about
their views on the case. In their discussions, they all decided
they were basically in agreement with what may have happened.
Cal believed the case had been mishandled. He believed the
convicted men could possibly be innocent. Cal even wrote a
forward for *The Monfils Conspiracy*. I admired him for his objec-
tivity and honesty.

Johnny had driven us over in his twenty-eight-foot RV,
equipped with bath, mini kitchen, and sleeping quarters. He and

Linda had bought it for family trips, but Johnny used it often as an office space for his ongoing investigation. It was a convenient place to conduct interviews. Inside John's house, we sat around the dining room table as our discussion got underway. After we listened to Bruce's artistic vision for a screenplay and shared our viewpoints, Johnny asked Cal to accompany him to his RV. After a while, Johnny returned and asked Byron to join him and Cal. When they returned, I noticed Johnny looked agitated. He was quieter than usual.

Johnny confided in me later. "You're not going to believe what I found out," he said. The intense look on his face told me this was big.

"I'm listening," I replied.

"Cal told me about a conversation he had with Detective Randy Winkler early in the investigation, regarding the knots used in the rope found around his brother's neck. Winkler had shown him photos of the rope and weight, and when he did, Cal told Winkler the knots in the picture looked like knots his brother would have tied. Then he said Winkler assured him this idea had been considered, but it was determined that the knots were not tied by his brother. Cal told Johnny he felt uncertain about what Winkler had said and shared his concerns that the photos were important because they were the only evidence he knew of that the prosecution had."

I was stunned. "No way," I said.

"Wait, there's more," Johnny said. He paused, sighing deeply before dropping another bomb. "Cal also told me about a conversation that took place at his parents' house shortly after the body was found. He said Tom's wife, Susan, told their (Cal and Tom's) parents she believed Tom committed suicide. Cal said his mother dismissed the idea as nonsense. But if this information was disclosed, it could bring new life to the entire case!"

Johnny's voice rose to a familiar high pitch as he continued. "See, this is what I keep saying. Damn it anyway! These were things that should have been brought up during the trial! Where the hell were the lawyers? They should have known these things and been all over them. This would have debunked the prosecution's murder theory. The jury would never have been able to convict because of the reasonable doubt that would have been raised. This could have cleared these men! Look, this case has nothing to do with murder. It was a suicide, plain and simple! The guy jumped in the vat! I was convinced of that from the get-go, and this proves it!"

Johnny had predicted something like this would happen, that crucial evidence would surface. He had said as much at the Oneida Nation High School in front of the family members. This was it, and it drove him mad because of another concern. "We have an even bigger dilemma," he said. "We can't do anything with this information right now, because Cal did not say these things under oath." Johnny explained, "In order for it to be legally binding, Cal will need to give a deposition. A lawyer will have to interview him and he'll have to sign a statement. Until then, the only thing we can do is sit on it until we find someone who is qualified to handle this. Oh, and one other thing, you cannot discuss this with anyone. Not even Clare."

My heart sank. I wanted to scream it from a rooftop, or, better yet, disclose it to the press. But Johnny was firm about keeping it quiet. "We need to go through the proper channels and do this right. That was not done the first time," he said. I knew he was right, but it was still one of the toughest things I've ever been asked to do. "You can only tell your husband but no one else can know. We cannot risk the backlash of too many people finding out."

Keeping this from my sister felt like a betrayal of her trust. So I approached this predicament by having a frank discussion with her and apologizing for not being able to say a word about this to her.

"That's okay if you cannot tell me," she said. "If it means helping Rey and the others, I don't want to know."

23

THOUGHTFUL SENTIMENTS

B y this time, Johnny had built a treasure trove of information about the case—videotapes of the crime scene, autopsy reports, various photos, witness statements, detail sheets from the original investigation, and many related documents. If it was accessible, he acquired it. He continued with interviews with former mill workers and family members. He searched online for news clips about the case. He poured himself into finding the one thing to prove these men were innocent. He had spent many hours digging deep, compiling and reviewing stacks of files, looking for a single key piece of tangible evidence to blow the lid off this case. Now he had it, from the most unlikely source.

From his standpoint, the admission from Cal was beyond significant, and it was an indication there was more to be discovered. "If that was never disclosed, what else were they hiding?" Johnny said. "If you smell one rat, there's always more."

Even though we were armed with this new information, Johnny was convinced it would not persuade any attorneys from the Green Bay area to get involved. "Nobody over there is going to touch this case. It's too controversial. We'll have to keep searching here in Minneapolis for someone whose judgment is not clouded."

We both knew it was a long shot to find a lawyer who would take this case but we had to keep trying. Johnny felt confident we'd be successful, but he was also cautious. "Whoever we find will have their work cut out for them," he said. "The work I've done is merely the tip of the iceberg."

I remember problem-solving with Johnny one day in our family room. We were feeling especially depressed because of the lack of options. The euphoria of uncovering this new evidence kept us hopeful, but we still had the lagging monetary problem. "That's always the deal-breaker for lawyers," Johnny said. "As soon as the discussion about money comes up, that's the end of it. Everyone wants to get paid. It's understandable, but frustrating as hell." We sat there saying little as we again sipped tea. I hardly tasted its mild burst of sweetness as I focused on the bitter reality this could be the end of the road. Neither of us wanted to believe it, and talking about it helped.

"We cannot hire just any attorney," I said. "It will have to be someone sympathetic who understands wrongful convictions, and whose best interests will rest on the welfare of the men."

I paused to think about something my mom used to say to us kids. It made me smile and seemed appropriate given the slump we were in. "When I was little, my mom piled all of us kids in the car and took us on an adventure," I said. "She was a new driver, so we could always count on her getting lost. She'd act like it was no big deal, and then laugh while declaring, 'I know where I'm going, I just don't know how to get there.' We'd get so mad at her, but now it's funny to think of her carefree attitude." This sparked a good laugh between us. Even in our doldrums, we could find something to brighten our spirits and make us feel like nothing was going to defeat us. With renewed vigor and a stubborn determination to succeed, we put our thinking caps back on.

A connection I had made previously dawned on me. "Remember me telling you I contacted someone from the Innocence Project of Minnesota when we had the book signing catastrophe during that stormy weekend?" I said. "They did respond to the e-mail I had sent, so maybe I should contact them again."

We decided it was worth a try. "Maybe they can give us some direction," said Johnny. "Maybe even some leads on attorneys."

24

VITAL CONNECTION

In 2012, I reached out to the IPMN a second time. Except now I felt more educated and more equipped to have a constructive conversation with them. This time I'd find out what they did, who they represented, and if they could enlighten us about a suitable attorney.

I sent a general e-mail again, inquiring about a visit to their office. "Can anyone just pop in?" I wrote. I included my phone number in the message. I received an e-mail, again from Julie Jonas. In her message, she included Erika Appelbaum, the executive director.

Erika decided to call me rather than communicate through e-mail. "What can I help you with?" she asked.

"My friend and I want to learn about the organization and meet your staff," I said. "We also want to share our story, and hopefully get some advice." I explained our predicament. Erika was surprised, but impressed that we'd taken on this mission. She stated how unusual it was for outsiders to get involved in something that didn't affect them personally. We became fast friends when we learned of our mutual acquaintance with Byron Lichstein and we set a date for a visit.

The front desk was vacant when Johnny and I entered the office. We peeked down the hallway as someone walked by. A young woman, an intern for the IPMN, acknowledged us. "We're here to see Erika," I said. The woman disappeared down the hall.

Erika soon emerged. Her face lit up when she saw us. "Come on back," she smiled, motioning for us to follow her. We reached her office and after some light chitchat, Erika asked about the Monfils case.

We shared most everything—our frustrations about the book signings, the failed search for legal assistance, and Byron's involvement in the efforts on Rey's behalf. We said nothing about what Cal had told Johnny. Erika was sympathetic but explained the IPMN was understaffed and backlogged with cases, which prevented them from helping us. However, it was a relief to share our woes with someone who understood our angst.

Julie Jonas took a quick break and came over. It was great to finally meet her in person. As the IPMN legal director, Julie was friendly but a bit more unassuming. She was fascinated with the court-related aspects of the case. She reluctantly returned to work before hearing the complete story but as she walked away, she mentioned an upcoming gala called a Benefit for Innocence. "You both should think about coming," she said. "Maybe you will meet some attorneys who can help."

Erika filled us in on those details and said it was scheduled for the fall. "Hundreds of guests, including attorneys, judges, media personalities, and more will be attending," she said. "An event page will be up on our website soon." She urged us to watch for it.

We thanked Erika for her time. Although we were disappointed they could not offer their services, we were hopeful about the event. "I think they would've helped us if they could," I said. "They seemed genuinely concerned about our situation."

Johnny agreed. I observed his excitement through the additional bounce in his step as we walked to his truck. Our euphoria could be seen by passersby as we drove north on Snelling Avenue in St. Paul. We cheered loudly and did high-fives. It didn't take much to get us going. "What would Linda and Mike think of us right now?" I said.

Johnny replied, "Who cares? I'm too excited to care." We laughed because we both knew Linda and Mike believed in us and in our mission and we could always count on them for helpful feedback. We both were eager to tell them about this new adventure.

25

DOSE OF REALITY

I watched for the 2012 Benefit for Innocence listing on the IPMN website. When it appeared, the information said it was scheduled for October eleventh at the (former) Graves Hotel in Minneapolis. The keynote speaker listed was someone named Damien Echols. I made a note to myself to read up on him.

We wanted to invite a few family members from Green Bay, but the event costs were prohibitive. However, exonerees received free admission. That at least meant Mike Pie could attend.

In a conversation with Mike Pie, he agreed to go and asked a favor of me. "Since you are signing us all up, could you invite some friends of mine? I think they'd come. They are fellow Wisconsin exonerees, Audrey Edmunds and Fred Saecker. It would be great to see them again."

We discussed overnight accommodations. "Johnny says you can stay at his place but do you think Audrey and Fred would feel comfortable staying with us?"

"I don't know, but you can ask them," Mike Pie said. "Fred's kind of quiet, but he's a really good guy and I think he'd be okay with that."

"What's Audrey like?" I asked.

"Audrey's easygoing and has a positive attitude," he said. "I'm sure you girls will get along great."

I took Mike Pie's advice and contacted Audrey and Fred. They responded, saying they planned to come. In his e-mail, Fred said he appreciated the offer to stay at our house. "You are kind by making this trip affordable for me," he wrote.

Fred seemed thoughtful and polite. I was shocked when I looked up his name online and read about his traumatic experience. Mike sat on the couch reading the newspaper as I searched the Internet for information. Numerous articles popped up as soon as I typed in Fred's name. "Mike, listen to this," I said. "Fred, the guy I just invited to stay with us, went to prison for burglary, second-degree sexual assault, and kidnapping!" We both thought light of it but, honestly, if we told others who were not familiar with wrongful convictions, they'd think we were off our rocker. "It says a woman was kidnapped from her home, raped, and abandoned on the side of a road in Bluff Siding, Wisconsin. The cops arrested Fred even though he didn't fit the description given by the victim, but because he was in her neighborhood. It says Fred is six feet, three inches tall. Even you'll be looking up to him," I teased.

During Fred's trial a truck driver testified to seeing Fred with a bloodstained T-shirt. A forensic analyst also testified pubic hairs found on the victim were "microscopically similar" to Fred's. "What does that mean?" I wondered. "'Microscopically' just means it was invisible or indistinct without the use of a microscope. So, it was small, but similar? How was that conclusive?"

I read more and discovered in 1993 Fred's mother paid for DNA testing, which excluded him as the perpetrator, but his request for a new trial was still denied. It wasn't until 1996, three years later, when the DA dismissed all charges based on this DNA evidence. "Why on earth did it take so long?" I thought. I felt sorry for a guy I hadn't met yet. How do you convict someone who's obviously the wrong guy? And where is the right guy? Did anyone ever think about that? I assumed the actual perpetrator was never arrested so he must still be out there.

Audrey said in her e-mail she lived about half an hour south of us, in Lakeville, Minnesota, so she'd meet us at the hotel the night of the event. Since she lived so close she wasn't sure if she'd spend the night.

I wondered about Audrey and her story. I was also curious about the number of female exonerees there were. According to the National Registry of Exonerations, founded in 2012 in conjunction with the Center on Wrongful Convictions at Northwestern University School of Law and the University of Michigan's Law School, which lists every known exoneration since 1989, it says, statistically, females make up about 9 percent of all wrongful convictions. Analysis from The Women's Project at the Center on Wrongful Convictions, shows false or misleading forensic evidence has played a role in more than a third of exonerated women's cases.

Many of these cases are also based on situational prosecutions where a female caregiver was blamed for someone's injury or death. About 43 percent of women exonerees have been convicted of harming or killing a child or loved one in their care. DNA evidence rarely proves their innocence, as it has in more than 25 percent of men's exonerations. DNA evidence has played a role in only 7 percent of women's exonerations.

In 1995, Audrey was married with three girls under the age of five. Their family lived in a small Wisconsin town called Waunakee. She ran an at-home daycare and, in October of that year, a baby fell ill at her house right after being dropped off. The baby died later that day, and an autopsy showed traumatic brain injuries. Audrey was convicted of first-degree reckless homicide, for Shaken Baby Syndrome (SBS). I'd heard about SBS. It was the same thing Louise Woodward, a nanny (referred to as an *au pair* in most news reports) from England who was working in Massachusetts, was charged with in 1997.

I tried to recall my impressions about the Woodward case, but couldn't remember any specifics, including what ultimately happened to her. So, I did some research and discovered a statement made by the police describing Woodward as saying she "popped the baby on the bed." There was a dispute in her case over the use of the word *popped* because in British English this term means "put" or "placed" rather than the more violence-oriented American English use. She claimed she was saying she "placed the baby on the bed." And, her defense lawyers argued to the jury the word *popped* does not have the same meaning as in American English. However, the police maintained she said she dropped him on the floor at one point and that she had been "a little rough" with him. The police officer who interviewed her immediately after the incident adamantly insists she never used the word *popped*, but in fact said she "dropped" the baby on the bed.

Based on this and other evidence, Woodward was convicted, but her sentence was reduced to time served (279 days), and she was freed. At a post-conviction relief hearing, the judge reduced the conviction to involuntary manslaughter, stating "the circumstances in which the defendant acted were characterized by confusion, inexperience, frustration, immaturity, and some anger, but not malice in the legal sense to support a conviction for second-degree murder." He added, "I am morally certain that allowing this defendant on this evidence to remain convicted of second-degree murder would be a miscarriage of justice."

It also said Woodward had asked for and passed a polygraph test before the trial. The most interesting aspect of this case was that her conviction effectively helped to defeat legislation in Massachusetts to restore capital punishment.

"Audrey was not so lucky," I said to Mike. "She was painted as a monster in court. It also says she was in prison for eleven years." Audrey had been given an eighteen-year sentence, but the Wisconsin Innocence Project secured her release in 2008. Interestingly, the same doctor whose testimony convicted her had also testified on her behalf when more factual information came to light about the symptoms present when a baby has been shaken. "It's a rare occurrence when an expert comes forth to admit they were wrong," I said. "It was fortunate for Audrey to have finally been freed but how sad for her girls to have essentially grown up without their mom."

By the time Audrey was released, her daughters were young adults. Her case is another instance where authorities didn't correctly determine what actually happened to the victim. And, the parents were never investigated despite the fact that old bruise marks which had already begun to heal were found on the baby's body when examined.

My husband Mike and I looked forward to meeting Audrey and Fred. "This is a bittersweet way to make an acquaintance," I said. "These people have gone to hell and back, and their circumstances are beyond anything I can comprehend. To imagine the trauma, the anger of being labeled as something they were not, to be called a sex offender, or baby killer, and then lose your freedom, is unfathomable to me. Mike Pie had been open, albeit emotional about his experience, but I wonder how easy it will be for these two to open up about theirs."

Audrey's story made me appreciate Jared's childhood, of how I did not have to worry about when I would see him again, or who was going to take care of him. "So, what do we say to them?" I said.

As always, Mike's advice was simple and practical. "Be honest," he said. "Tell them what you just told me."

In an earlier conversation, Mike Pie had shared what many exonerees face after being released. "They have no money to live on, and they either end up with low-paying jobs or none at all. Many find themselves without housing," he said. "People don't realize that job opportunities and government compensation are hard to come by, or nonexistent. Because of the beliefs about us being guilty, and the screwed-up way that compensation laws are set up, there are few payouts by the state."

How many times had I heard others say everyone in prison claims to be innocent, or an offender was released on a technicality? Consider this idea shared by IPMN legal director Julie Jonas. She argues it may actually be innocent people who are being kept in prison on technicalities unlawfully administered by authorities who resist an admission that mistakes have been made.

Uninformed attitudes from the public add to the problem, putting exonerees in the center of these unresolved controversies. "The injustices do not end just because we are released," Mike Pie said. "For many, it creates a whole new set of problems."

Mike Pie's statement alludes to a matter still being resolved between individual states, and those proven to have been wrongfully convicted—monetary compensation. On average, exonerees spend more than fourteen years behind bars. The agony of prison life and the complete loss of freedom are accompanied by thoughts about what their life might've been like without a wrongful conviction. The nightmare is compounded by years of deprivation from family and friends, and of the ability to establish oneself professionally. The feelings of complete loss don't end because the person is released. The exoneree still has to face the reality that he or she typically has no valid ID or driver's license, no money or bank account, no housing, no transportation, no health services or insurance, and is plagued with a prior criminal background, whether or not the wrongful conviction is removed from court records.

After these individuals have been freed, I believe states have a responsibility to restore their lives as best they can because of the difficulties they face when reentering society. Because they often have no funds available for basic necessities, failure to compensate them in this manner adds insult to injury. I feel it is our duty as a society to assist them. This can be achieved through a number of ways: 1) compensation through a set dollar amount for each year spent in prison; 2) providing access to services like basic housing, medical/dental care (that was substandard or nonexistent in prison), counseling, assistance with education, job counseling and training, and legal services (to assist them with expungement of their criminal records and regaining custody of their children); and 3) a means of obtaining public benefits (since compensation has to be applied for, and wrongly accused often must prove actual innocence in order to receive it).

The admission by the government that no system is perfect and that it's willing to take responsibility for its wrongs or errors, and public recognition of the harm inflicted upon a wrongfully convicted person, helps to foster healing. To date, the federal government, the District of Columbia, and thirty states have compensation statutes. These twenty states don't: Alaska, Arizona, Arkansas, Delaware, Georgia, Hawaii, Idaho, Indiana,

Kansas, Kentucky, Michigan, Nevada, New Mexico, North Dakota, Oregon, Pennsylvania, Rhode Island, South Carolina, South Dakota, and Wyoming.

Each state that does offer monetary compensation determines the conditions that must be met and the specific amount. Compensation packages range from $5,000/year, with a cap of $25,000 in Wisconsin, to $80,000/year in Texas, along with a matching annuity. President George W. Bush endorsed an overall recommendation by Congress of $50,000/year, with an additional $50,000 for each year spent on death row. But many exonerees don't receive anything because of the opposition from law enforcement and the legal obstacles to obtain it.

Many exonerees resort to filing lawsuits against the State upon release. One example of a large settlement awarded to an exoneree is the case of Jeffrey Deskovic from New York. He was wrongfully convicted of rape and murder in 1990 at age seventeen, and remained in prison until 2006. DNA evidence helped to overturn his conviction. He filed a lawsuit and was awarded a settlement of $41.2 million. He used those funds to start The Jeffrey Deskovic Foundation, which educates the public about wrongful convictions and helps others who have been wrongly imprisoned.

A sad commentary of these injustices is highlighted in Deskovic's case. He was convicted despite DNA results showing he was not the source of semen in the victim's rape kit. The state got around that fact by arguing the semen had come from a consensual sex partner and that Deskovic killed the victim in a jealous rage. When he was exonerated, the DNA was tested again. This identified the real perpetrator, who was in prison for a later murder. So, by convicting the wrong person, another murder that should have been prevented was allowed to happen.

26

GRAVE TESTIMONIALS

Mike came home from work early the day of the benefit in time to help greet our guest. We knew nothing about Fred other than what Mike Pie had said and what I'd found online.

Fred's most distinct characteristic was his height. Like in articles describing him, Fred was tall, and thin. But neither his size nor his nature was domineering. Rather, he was soft spoken, shy, and humble. "I struggle with being in large groups," Fred admitted. "But I wanted to come to this event so I could see my good friends, Mike Pie and Audrey. I don't get to see them very often." Fred then asked, "Did Mike Pie tell you about my situation?"

"Not too much," I said. "But I looked it up online." Fred seemed at ease with us as he talked at length about his experience from the past.

"The authorities are not always interested in going after the truth," he said. "Look at the description of the perp in my case. It wasn't even close to what I look like. But that didn't matter. They arrested, charged, and convicted me anyway."

I saw many similarities in both Fred with Mike Pie. Neither of them seemed capable of committing the heinous crimes for which they were convicted. In fact, they both exhibited genuine, unselfish, and sincere attributes. Like Mike Pie, Fred still harbored mistrust for the authorities, which was the basis for his concern of others he'd met while in prison. "I'm grateful for my freedom," he said. "But I know lots of innocent guys who are still in prison.

In fact, the prisons are full of them, and it makes me sad to think of how many will never have their cases looked into."

Before long, we heard another vehicle pull up to the house. Johnny, Linda, and Mike Pie appeared. They were all decked out. Mike Pie was wearing a suit he borrowed from Johnny. "Wow, don't you look respectable," I said.

"Not too shabby," said Mike Pie as they walked in.

Johnny spotted Fred and gave him the once-over. "I don't think I have anything to fit you, Fred," Johnny teased as he turned his head upward to look Fred in the eyes.

"I'm okay wearing what I have on," said Fred. The two chuckled as they shook hands.

Fred definitely towered over Johnny's short and stocky frame. "Hmmm…Mutt and Jeff," I said. Everyone laughed, giving Johnny the audience he craved and the attention he loved. And we all, of course, loved his antics. He was stimulating, but he could also effectively work a room.

Off we went on this new adventure. On the way out, I grabbed a tote bag filled with gifts I had packed earlier. When I began meeting exonerees who were forced to live in small cells for years at a time, I thought they might enjoy reading my son's book about being in the open wilderness and the freedom to go wherever they pleased. I felt this event was the perfect place to hand them out.

During the ride to the hotel, I sat back and observed Fred. You'd never guess his traumatic past by looking at him. Exonerees resemble all of us. They could be the neighbor mowing their lawn, the person shopping at the grocery store, or someone riding down the street on a bike. You'll never know if and when you'll cross paths. I thought they'd stand out for some reason, but they don't. You feel uneasy when you realize what happened to them can happen to any of us. I wondered how I had been so ignorant about wrongful convictions, and about the number of people affected by them.

We picked up Jared's friend, Erik Stewart (who'd read the Monfils book and begun exchanging letters with Keith Kutska), on the way to the event. We were also meeting Tori, one of my coworkers, in the lobby of the hotel. We entered a spacious room and headed toward the sign-in desk.

My husband was amused at the sight of me with my big tote bag of books swinging from my shoulder. "Let me carry those," he said as he smiled.

Tori waved to us. Her temperament was similar to Johnny's boisterous and outspoken nature, and she could also pour on lighthearted sarcasm. "Well…where have you been?" she joked. "I've been waiting for hours. Honestly, I have better things to do than to wait around all day." She then turned serious. "I can't wait to meet Audrey," she said. "She is coming, right?"

"I hope so," I said. "I don't see her in the lobby. Maybe she's in the reception room."

We found the elevator and ascended upward. When the doors opened we entered a large room with people standing in small groups. I immediately spotted Audrey. There was no mistaking her. She was tall, slim, blonde, and beautiful, like in pictures I'd seen of her online after her release. She was talking to a Hmong couple. Tori and I separated from the others and approached them. I touched Audrey's arm. She turned and guessed who I was. We hugged, and I introduced Tori to her. She then introduced us to the couple standing there. Panghoua Moua and Koua Fong Lee smiled and nodded. Audrey introduced us to Koua who was also an exoneree.

In June of 2006, Koua Fong Lee was driving his family home from church. While on an exit ramp in St. Paul, Minnesota, the 1996 Toyota Camry he was driving accelerated out of control. It reached a speed of ninety miles an hour, crashing into a stopped car in front of them. Three people were killed and two others were injured. In 2007, Koua was charged with intentional vehicular homicide and sentenced to eight years in prison. Two years into his sentence, more Toyota drivers reported similar acceleration issues. Toyota started to recall millions of cars, but not the 1996 model. Based on this new evidence and errors by his trial lawyer, Koua filed a motion for a new trial. The lawyers representing Toyota fought the motion, claiming his vehicle was not flawed. But Koua was granted a new trial and he was exonerated in August of 2010, after serving three years of his sentence. In this case, there was no unseen perpetrator, just a trail of lasting devastation for his family and the families of the decedents.

I saw unmistakable humility in this couple, and how this man had been bullied due to his trusting nature. When we believe people are similar to us we drop our guard. However, some people take advantage of that goodwill. Even after his frightening experience Koua still emphasizes the good in others. "We are very grateful for the help we receive from many good people," he said.

Theirs was and is a perplexing battle. In ongoing efforts to receive monetary compensation from a resistant automotive company, Koua and his family have fought for normalcy as they raise four beautiful children. Having seen Koua and Panghoua on many occasions since, the trauma they've experienced is still evident.

Tori and I excused ourselves to catch up with the others who were gathered around another exoneree named Damon Thibodeaux. We were introduced to Damon and learned he had been released a week prior to this event. He was quiet but responsive, and I soon learned he's the same age as my son. For that reason alone, I found it difficult to stomach his disturbing story.

In July of 1996 Damon was a twenty-two-year-old deckhand on a Mississippi River barge in New Orleans, Louisiana. During that month, his stepcousin was found strangled to death. He aided in a search to find her before being brought in for questioning. Already exhausted, Damon was questioned for nine hours. Due to police pressure, intimidation, and being threatened with the death penalty, he falsely confessed to raping and murdering his cousin.

The case against him was built upon this confession even though there were discrepancies in his statement. For example, his confession of rape was ludicrous since there was no physical evidence a rape had even occurred. However, this fact did not stop the authorities from including it in the charges brought against him.

Damon had also been misidentified. A week after the crime, two women picked him out of a photo lineup. At the trial, they pointed to him as the perpetrator. However, during a later investigation of his case it was revealed the women had seen Damon's face on the news prior to identifying him in the photo lineup. Additionally, the date they claimed to have seen him on was incorrect because he was already in custody by then.

Damon spent fifteen years on death row in one of the country's worst prisons, Louisiana's Angola Prison. He was isolated in an 8x10-foot cell for twenty-three hours a day. He is the three hundredth person nationwide, and the eighteenth from death row, to be exonerated by DNA evidence. He was released in September of 2012 and, again, the true perpetrator was never sought out.

Standing near Damon was an attorney from the Minneapolis law firm of Fredrikson & Byron, PA. And beside both of them, talking up a storm, was Johnny. The firm is known for its generosity in contributing pro bono services to clients and nonprofits in the Minneapolis area. And like I said earlier, Johnny has a keen ability to work a room and an eye for picking the right person out of a crowd at the right time. So I was curious to meet this attorney.

I approached them. "Hey Joan, this is Steve Kaplan," Johnny explained. "He was instrumental in helping with Damon's exoneration. I've been telling him about the Monfils case."

Steve was soft spoken and charming. He talked about Damon with pride, about spending the last twelve years working on this case, his relief that it was over and that Damon was free. It was inspiring to hear such dedication toward his client, and I wondered if we could find someone like him to help us.

About halfway through the reception Damien Echols, the keynote speaker for the evening, appeared alongside his wife, Lorri. He was distinguishable in his dark glasses and long jacket, similar to a trench coat, which was a typical portrayal of him on various social media sites. Lorri was striking with deep blue eyes and a bright smile. They both stood in the center of the room as a crowd slowly surrounded them.

With my son's book in hand, I waited my turn to speak with them. Damien had a calming effect on those around him. He was personable and relaxed. Lorri was more outgoing socially. I was familiar with their story through watching a three-part documentary called *Paradise Lost*, which detailed the case in which Echols and two other boys were involved.

Three teenage boys, Damien Echols, Jessie Misskelley Jr., and Jason Baldwin, were convicted of murdering three eight-year-old Cub Scout boys in West Memphis, Arkansas, in 1994. Echols, Misskelley, and Baldwin were dubbed "The West Memphis Three." Echols, the main suspect, received three death penalties. Baldwin and Misskelley (who had an IQ of 68) were given life sentences despite no physical evidence linking any of them to the crime. The authorities failed to pursue every possible lead and they fabricated evidence, even enhanced the storyline, labeling the deaths as satanic killings to terrify and infuriate a prejudiced community.

I found the films compelling and fascinating because of the distinct similarities to the Monfils case. Echols was someone who was seen as a troublemaker, like Keith Kutska. The platform of public opinion had all three boys charged, tried, and sentenced before any of them saw the inside of a courtroom. Finger-pointing and cruel epithets were aimed at them from every direction despite no evidence tying them to these murders. And as though it carried significant weight, the boys were mischaracterized and accused of being involved in satanic rituals and human sacrifice simply because they wore black clothing and listened to heavy metal music.

Although watching the documentary series leads us to speculate about other possible suspects, no one else has ever been investigated or charged. To this day, reasonable doubt about the guilt of these three men remains high, yet the police have shown no interest in seeking out the real murderer.

This case introduces a disturbing aspect of the criminal justice process. Years into their sentences, all three of these boys agreed to change their original pleas from not guilty, to guilty, in exchange for immediate release. This is known as an Alford Plea.

It's a legal maneuver allowing someone to maintain his or her innocence while acknowledging the likelihood that prosecutors have enough evidence to convict. It's an option also offered to potential exonerees when they are faced with the prospect of a new trial. According to Echols, it was his only option because of his inability to survive in prison any longer. For him, it was literally the difference between life and death. Some see an Alford Plea as a source of worry due to the implications it places on overall exonerations. I see it as another way of bullying innocents, of maintaining control over their fates, and a last-ditch attempt to satisfy a prosecutor's position before releasing an inmate.

Echols had spent eighteen years in prison and refers to that experience, and his legal battle for freedom, as an "absolute living hell." In 2012, he published a memoir called *Life After Death*. He had brought books along with him that evening to sell.

By the time my turn came to speak with Damien, Lorri was elsewhere talking to other attendees. I offered him a copy of Jared's book. "This is for you," I said. "My son wrote it. I'd like you to have it."

He was delighted to receive it. "Thank you," he said.

"I'm deeply sorry for what you've been through," I said.

Damien explained the dark glasses he wore. "My eyesight was destroyed from being in a small, dark room for so many years," he said. It was heartbreaking to hear.

We covered a few lighter topics before I asked, "Could we have our picture taken together?"

"Sure," he said, "but no one can use a flash."

We searched for a spot with suitable lighting. I worried Damien might be irritated when it took longer than expected, but he wasn't. As we stood there posing I felt Damien's hand touch my shoulder, as if to calm my worries.

I spoke with Lorri later on. She was open about her deep love for this man and is modest about her role in this devastating story. Her story is one of redemption and how she helped to lift Damien out of the depths of despair while he was in prison. They had started a relationship through letters that developed into marriage while Damien was still incarcerated. It was a situation that called for great courage and devotion on both sides. I gathered it was because of her compassion that Damien was liberated from his hell on earth.

After meeting everyone, we entered a dining hall filled with white linen tables. Hundreds of guests were in attendance. The atmosphere was energized by laughter and conversation. Audrey, Fred, and Mike Pie joined us at our table. In fact, we received favorable mention for having the most exonerees at a single table.

Afterward, it was time for Damien's talk. He did not give a speech but opted for a more relaxed Q&A led by a moderator. It was eye-opening, touching, and infuriating to hear about the hate he experienced from a prejudiced community, a biased judicial process, and the constant beatings and years of isolation while on death row. His reality was inconceivable, and sighs of disbelief could be heard throughout the room as he described his traumatic experience. Once you hear these things, they never escape you. If you care enough, you'll never dismiss them, and if you are smart enough, you'll never forget them.

After dinner, an announcement was made. A table was set up just outside the dining hall for those who had not yet purchased Damien's book. Linda leaned over and said, "Joan, let's go and buy our copies." This gave us a chance to also express our sincere sorrow for what Damien went through, and to thank him for sharing his story. We wished the best for both him and Lorri before returning to the dining hall.

We found the others and gravitated toward a crowd surrounding a young man named Mike Hansen. He's a client of the IPMN who was exonerated in 2011. Hansen looked young. At the very least, his wrongful conviction had not stolen his youth. He was fortunate to have many years ahead to create a new life and a new future. His shaved head resembled my son's, and his face lit up when he laughed. He was quite self-assured and seized the attention of those around him. He looked each of us in the eye as he offered a firm handshake. His story was similar to Audrey's and, as he talked about it, his narration was accompanied by a

definite scolding aimed at the authorities who had caused catastrophic harm to him and his family years earlier.

In 2006, Michael Hansen was convicted of murdering his
three-month-old daughter, Avryonna. On the morning of her
death, he had found her unresponsive. He called 911, but she
could not be revived. An autopsy was performed and the medical examiner testified at his trial that the infant died of a skull
fracture from an intentional blow to the head, even though he
found little evidence of swelling, bleeding, or brain injuries. He
dismissed the idea that the fracture could've been caused by
a fall she took from a shopping cart six days prior to her death.

The case was reopened by the IPMN, and they hired a team
of experts to reevaluate the autopsy. These experts testified a
skull fracture alone does not cause death and that it must be
accompanied by underlying bleeding or some type of brain
injury before death can occur in an infant. It was determined
Avryonna most likely died of accidental suffocation or sudden
infant death syndrome (SIDS) while sleeping. Hansen served five
and a half years of a fourteen-and-a-half-year sentence before
the charges against him were formally dismissed.

Despite convincing research, there is much dissention and
debate in the scientific world about the circumstances surrounding infant deaths, leaving parents desperate to find peace
with the death of their child. Often, parents are sent to prison or
face separation from their children when genetic anomalies are
present and misdiagnosed. Osteogenesis imperfecta is a group
of genetic disorders mainly affecting the bones, causing imperfect bone formation or frequent breakage due to mild trauma, or,
in many cases, no apparent reason. Often, cases of osteogenesis
imperfecta are mistaken for child abuse. The 2016 film titled *The
Syndrome* and other similar documentaries seeking to address
SBS (featuring cases like Audrey's) are being created and used
to educate the public on the latest facts.

As we drove home from the benefit, the car was quiet but
my mind was buzzing. Johnny, Linda, and Mike Pie agreed to
stop over for a nightcap. This was welcomed because I needed
to decompress from what I'd seen and heard. At some point

during the evening I realized all the exonerees we'd met had one thing in common—none of them appeared angry. I found this odd. These situations were beyond horrible, so how could they be so cheerful, so calm, and so damned peaceful?

Family members I've talked to over the years with loved ones in prison for crimes they did not commit have their own set of worries. Jenny, Keith Kutska's niece, whose outspoken nature matches that of her uncle, puts it this way: "There are some family members who won't mention him anymore, as if he fell off the face of the earth. That is what breaks my heart. The ones that miss him are the ones who have lost out, not to mention Keith himself, who has been robbed of his absolute freedom. His name has been dragged through the dirt. Those who didn't truly know him thank God for sending such a 'beast of a man' to prison. That pains me as well. And his reputation as a wonderful man is forever shattered even if he is found innocent. People are going to hear the name Keith Kutska and cringe because of the mess up in the judicial system. His life will never be the same. When the day comes that God decides it's his time to die, and I pray it's not soon, I will bawl my eyes out, as will his family. I just want to scream to the world—he's not who you think he is! He's not a murderer! But my fear is that no one will listen."

Jenny's "beast of a man" quote compelled me to search online for a possible reference. That search led me to an article in the *Deseret News* out of Utah, dated October 29, 1995. In the article, District Attorney John Zakowski had highlighted a quote by Ralph Waldo Emerson in reference to the Monfils case stating, "A mob is man descending to the level of beast."

This benefit was about people traumatized unnecessarily within a criminal justice system that had failed them and all of us, by shattering the ideals, the hopes, and the dreams by which we all live. But for those we met, miraculous changes had occurred. They were fortunate to be free. And they knew it. Because of their good fortune they were making peace with their circumstances. I wondered why it had happened to them and not me. But there seemed to be a common theme among those I spoke with—trying to reconcile our imperfect criminal justice system and why it tolerates wrongful convictions even in the face of compelling evidence of innocence.

I thought about Damien and his plea deal. Though this wasn't an ideal option, it was the only viable one for him at the time. And he seemed content for the time being for the freedom it allowed him, at least until he could find a way to achieve formal exoneration. Damien also knew how lucky he was to be liberated from death row with the help of the Innocence Project of New York and a remarkable legal team. Audrey and Mike Hansen expressed gratefulness for the guidance they received through the Minnesota and Wisconsin Innocence Projects and new scientific advances. Fred had the benefit of DNA testing and Koua received enough support through collective information from other victims and advocates alike, prompting new legal action.

But now the challenges for them were more about survival on the outside, in a whole new world. The most important thing they'd have to rely on was the support of family and true friends who could pull them through difficult times ahead.

As uplifting as this event was, the reality of what we lacked in our mission was still quite real for our five incarcerated men. There was no DNA. The Wisconsin Innocence Project had recently lost an appeal for Rey Moore, and there were no new appeals on the horizon. Because of the lack of any direct evidence of homicide, there are no obvious perpetrators or witnesses. Our biggest hurdle remained the absence of funds to pay an exceptional and willing attorney. Three years into this and we'd barely made it out of the starting gate. The constant stress and urgency about the unsettled future of our case weighed heavily on my mind. The stories we heard that evening all proved goodness prevailed through miracles, but where was ours?

27

A GATHERING OF FRIENDS

After the Benefit for Innocence, Audrey and I met for lunch occasionally. Her free spirit, strength, and her ability to wear a smile despite her circumstances were attributes that inspired me to reject the negativity in my life, and embrace only the positive. My husband always says it best when he describes Audrey as "one of the most positive people he has ever met."

Our first lunch date was before Thanksgiving in 2012. It was then that Audrey told me about a book she was writing. "It's called *It Happened to Audrey: It Could Happen to You*," she said. "It'll be published soon."

"I'd like to have a copy," I said. Knowing about her book gave me a great idea. "Can I host a book signing for you at my house?" I asked.

Audrey was delighted. "You'd do that for me?" she asked.

"Of course. I think we should schedule it for early December before everyone is bombarded with Christmas activities," I said. "Mike and I will even set out some holiday goodies."

On December 8, 2012, Mike and I hosted a gathering of approximately twenty people at our house. Beforehand, I'd sent online invitations to a few close friends, as well as to Erika and Julie from the IPMN. Although I was unsure if Steve Kaplan would remember me after such a brief introduction at the benefit, I decided to send an invitation to him and his wife, Norma. I also extended their invitation to include Damon. Responses came back, and the turnout was looking great. Then, the one response I waited for appeared.

An e-mail from Steve came with good news. He had accepted the invitation and, although Norma could not come, he planned to bring Damon. Steve also asked about inviting one other person. After sending my reply, I told Johnny, "Steve remembered me."

"Well, of course he did," he said. "Joan, I told you before. I keep tellin' you. You have this ability to get people's attention, and now you have Steve Kaplan's. Someday you'll learn there isn't anything you can't do."

The majority of those we invited came, but Johnny had the flu so he and Linda stayed home. Steve and Damon were among the last to arrive. I noticed a positive change in Damon since the benefit. He seemed at ease with more confidence. He conversed with the other guests, and we learned he possessed a hearty laugh. He was doing great, considering he'd spent the past fifteen years in solitary confinement. Since his release, he was living with the Kaplans so he could focus on getting his GED. I admired that level of kindness and thought it uncommon. Their generosity was setting this young man up for success.

When Damon completed his studies, we were invited to his high school graduation. He was all smiles that night. He went on to enroll in commercial truck driving school, and now he spends his days on the open road as a professional truck driver, something he used to dream about in a tiny cell.

Steve introduced me to Pam Wandzel, the person he had asked to bring. Pam is the director of the Pro Bono and Community Services program at the law firm. We chatted briefly before Mike reminded me of the time. "We should get Audrey's presentation started," he said.

"We can talk later," Steve remarked.

Everyone sat down, and before I could formally introduce Audrey, she greeted the crowd from her seat at the large table. "This woman needs no introduction," I thought. So I quickly grabbed a plate of food and joined the other guests.

Audrey was as delightful as her story was disheartening. We all listened as horrific details emerged about her experience.

Most disturbing was her description of being separated from her three daughters and how she worried about their well-being while she was "away." Audrey uses noncommittal words like that because, in her mind, she never allowed herself to become a prisoner. She never catered to being a number, and she never gave up on the idea of someday being released. In the meantime, she maintained a normal routine as best she could, with exercise and a healthy diet. She saw the devastation happening to other women around her who abused themselves with drugs, cigarettes, junk food, and a lack of exercise. She avoided any type of violence, and was thankful she was never threatened.

The mood in the room was somber as she illustrated how someone as kind, gentle, and loving as she had been bullied and labeled a monster in court. Her experience resembled four primary themes in all wrongful convictions: 1) unwarranted character defamation; 2) an incomplete or inaccurate depiction of what happened; 3) neglect by law enforcement to look into all possible suspects; and 4) narrowly focusing on a specific person despite evidence that proves their innocence. When Audrey finished, the group applauded her efforts of sharing her nightmare, knowing it took great courage to relive it.

Then my friend and coworker Candee spoke up. "I'm not familiar with Damon's story. I was wondering if it's okay for him to talk about his experience."

Everyone liked the idea and, with a little encouragement, Damon also shared details of his circumstances. He talked about confessing to a crime he did not commit. "Until you've been placed in a situation where you are coerced into confessing to something you didn't do, you cannot know how that feels," he said.

Over time I learned the rationale behind the absurdity of confessing to a crime you did not commit. Suspects are supposed to be interviewed but instead get interrogated, which is a more aggressive tactic known as the Reid Method of Interrogation. It's used by law enforcement when closing a case becomes more important than going after the truth. The suspects are fed lies. They are told they can go home or will get a better deal from the courts if they admit involvement. They are scolded and continually fed facts about the crime known only to the police and to the actual criminal. The interrogator will say, "We know you did this." They will confuse the suspect by saying they have a witness who has identified him or her as the perpetrator. This is terrifying to hear, especially when the suspect succumbs to exhaustion from the constant barrage of questions, and an inability to distinguish fact from fiction. In death penalty states, interrogators use that as leverage to coerce suspects into confessing. Suspects are told of the risks of putting their fate in the hands of an unsympathetic jury. Many are offered shorter sentences in exchange for a guilty plea.

Damon was threatened with the death penalty, which was ultimately given to him despite his confession. He talked about his experience on death row—the heat, the long days, and how it felt to be stared at as people from various tour groups consisting of religious groups, schoolchildren, and tourists taking side trips from their vacations, walked past his cell. He talked about how Steve Kaplan came into his life and became not only his lawyer but his friend and mentor, and his gratitude for consistent contact with Steve while his case was in litigation.

Afterward, I said to Damon, "I cannot begin to understand what you went through."

His reply to me was profound. "I hope you never do, because that will mean you didn't have to go through what I did."

To lighten the mood, I fetched gifts for our guests. I asked Damon to stay at the table while I ushered Audrey back up. "Since we are entering the harshest part of our Minnesota winter, I'm gracing each of you with a practical gift," I said as they pulled thick knitted hats from their gift bags. We shared hearty laughs as they each playfully donned them.

Damon remarked, "I definitely needed one of these." Afterward, we shared more laughter and hugs while Audrey signed books.

Time was slipping away and I still needed to talk to Steve about the Monfils case. I wished Johnny was there to help reiterate, in terms an attorney could better understand, why it was imperative this case be revisited. I knew enough about the case to answer basic questions about what happened and what evidence was used against them, but my lack of legal knowledge prevented me from taking on more complicated procedural ones about appeals and investigative procedures.

But no amount of knowledge could answer the one question Steve eventually asked: "Why was one released, and not the other five?"

I'd learned from Johnny that no attorney asks a question he doesn't know the answer to, but this one had no rational answer. "That is the big mystery," I said. "It should've ignited a reinvestigation into the case, but it didn't."

After a while, I broached the subject of legal assistance. I tread lightly. Since Steve had only recently finished with Damon's case, I felt it unwise to ask him outright to represent our men. And I had not forgotten about his plans to retire soon. Instead, I asked for any attorney recommendations he might have. He suggested I talk to Pam about making an appointment at the firm.

Pam advised me to call the office and set up an appointment. I told her I would. At this event, we'd been afforded something we wished for above all else for the longest time—an invitation to a sizeable law firm. I had done my part, now all Johnny had to do was go through the mountain of documentation he'd gathered over the past two years and decide what to bring along. I couldn't wait to give him the news.

28

UNLOADING A HEAVY BURDEN

Sometimes our plans took unexpected turns and we'd find ourselves scrambling to recover, like the day in January 2013 when Johnny and I were scheduled to meet with Pam Wandzel at Fredrikson & Byron, PA to discuss the Monfils case.

As Pam had indicated, I set up the appointment with her. The day arrived. Johnny drove. And we were lost in downtown Minneapolis which was the norm for both of us anytime we headed that way. After circling the block a few times we finally located the entrance to the underground parking garage, quickly found a parking space, and rushed toward our destination. We had managed to arrive with time to spare.

The firm itself is comprised of many floors in the US Bank Plaza building, with the reception desk being located on the fortieth floor. Johnny brought his large, heavy cardboard box full of case files along. After we made our way through the parking garage, the main floor plaza, and up the elevator he remarked, "There is no way I am carrying this box back home. That simply is non-negotiable."

As soon as we walked off the elevator, Johnny set the box down on a nearby coffee table with a thud. I approached the receptionist with a smile, and made light of the commotion behind me. "We're here to see Pam," I said. "She's expecting us."

We waited as she made the call. After she hung up, we received devastating news. "Pam is not in today due to an illness," she said. "Can you reschedule?"

Johnny and I looked at each other, panic setting in. I then leaned over to him and said, "We've been waiting for this appointment and we cannot leave without talking to someone. Hang on, I have an idea." I turned back to her and asked, "Is Steve Kaplan in today?"

She offered to check as she picked up the phone once again. We both crossed our fingers. As she hung up the receiver, she said, "Steve will be right down." I thanked her.

Johnny stated loudly, "I hope he remembers us."

I told him to hush. I joked to him about how embarrassing he could be sometimes. I thought fondly of his poor wife, Linda, and what she had to deal with on a daily basis. Johnny reveled in this new twist. "Way to go, Treppa," he whispered.

We both considered Steve a compassionate and generous lawyer, and speaking with him directly could be advantageous. We resisted getting our hopes up or appearing overly anxious about this prospect. I also hoped we were not upsetting Steve's busy schedule in his last month with the firm.

As we waited, we marveled at our surroundings. Large paintings of the firm's founders adorned the walls, and the view overlooking Minneapolis was stunning. The sheer size of the place was daunting. The audacity of expecting a firm this size to pay attention to us felt surreal. But there we stood, driven like desperados, equipped with nothing but a tattered box of documents and an unrivaled determination on behalf of individuals who had witnessed too many years of pain and sorrow.

But then the idea of us standing there in that lobby began to feel as if this was meant to be. An affirmation washed over me that miracles are real, and that our dreams could somehow come true.

I thought about how Steve had expressed his intrigue with the case. "Maybe he will decide to take it on," I thought. "It does need the attention of someone like him." But I also thought it silly to ask. My thoughts were interrupted as Steve exited the elevator and walked toward us. He greeted us with the warmth of old friends and we both felt the burden of our troubles diminish. As Steve quizzed the receptionist about an empty conference room,

Johnny and I caught each other's glance. We nodded in agreement that this was somehow going to work out just fine.

"You may use the second room on the left," replied the receptionist, and off we went. We talked for an hour, then two, and well into a third. Steve's professionalism and knowledge of the law allowed him to unravel the confusing details with which he was inundated. We were relieved to finally have an outlet to share our coveted information supporting a suicide theory.

Johnny explained everything he had discovered over the past two years and I shared my connections to the families, friends, and the five incarcerated men. I assured Steve of my ability to facilitate trust between them and whomever took the legal reins, and that they would welcome any endorsements we made. Johnny and I stressed our concerns about future mismanagement of the case because of the ineffective lawyers the families had dealt with in the past. I was ready to hire Steve Kaplan right then and there. All he had to do was say the word.

Before we wrapped up our meeting, we reluctantly declared there were no funds to pay an attorney. Steve still agreed to look at the paperwork Johnny had brought. We were grateful for his time and we walked out of the meeting feeling our concerns had been heard and understood. We said our good-byes and left, and we waited patiently for what we might hear back.

29

OVERCOMING
MAJOR HURDLES

Steve Kaplan retired in February of 2013. As much as we wished him well, we silently prayed he'd have good news for us to share with the families in Green Bay. Up to this point, we had refrained from saying anything to them about our meeting with Steve until we had an idea of the outcome, in case things did not work out.

While we waited, we tried to muster enthusiasm for a next move. The real possibility that our search was not over, persisted. As time passed with no word from Steve, our optimism slowly faded. We convinced ourselves that he was enjoying retirement too much to consider our proposal, and that the Damon Thibodeaux case was going to be the capstone on his well-deserved legacy. "He's not going to jump back into a big case like this," I said. "He's going to realize it's another long-term commitment."

Johnny countered those remarks with, "One never knows what he will do. Let's be patient a little longer." Even though I questioned Johnny's optimism, I felt hopeful that he was right. Aside from my certainty that Steve was the perfect candidate for this specific case, I questioned our rationale for believing he'd get involved, especially for free.

My dismay and sadness for the families grew. They'd be the losers if we failed to bring Steve or anyone else from the firm onboard. I kept reminding myself that Steve had alluded to contributing minimal assistance after he retired. It was not the preferred outcome but it was something to hold on to. But even the plausibility of that notion grew more unlikely as time passed. If he did decide to help us, how long would he let it invade his life? What if this case became overwhelming or was too time consuming? I wondered about the travel and unforeseen expenses along the way. I was certain if he did take it on he'd never find anyone to help him. There was no shaking my inner battle between optimism and apprehension. It was easy to get caught up in the moment during that productive meeting. There, anything had seemed possible. But reality was starting to set in. However, I clung to the fact that my persistence in book sales had produced desirable results, and I told myself we could achieve a similar result once again.

My faith in the impossible was confirmed one day as I turned on my computer to check e-mails. A message was there from Steve. I read furiously through to the end, looking for an indication of his intentions. There it was—verification that he was willing to help us! The words took a moment to sink in before I jumped up to call Johnny. "It took us two long years, but we've done it," I said.

"This changes everything," said Johnny. "Now we can see about getting this case back into the courts. I'm coming over. We have things to do. The first thing you should do is let the folks in Green Bay know, and have them organize a meeting at Shirley's."

I agreed. "I'll get an e-mail sent out right away," I said. "If the media gets wind of this, there's no telling how they might react and we don't want them to catch the families off guard."

One day, shortly after we'd gotten the e-mail from Steve, Johnny and I ran over to see Erika and Julie at the IPMN to share the good news. They had already been notified due to their association with the law firm, but it was still great to see them. They were kind and even though they were extremely busy, they'd always make time to visit with us. We spoke briefly with Erika, and as we walked back toward the front door to leave we passed Julie's office. We said a quick "hello" and she called us in to chat about the latest development. She appeared excited and asked many questions. Julie always showed interest in our ongoing activities. That day, she wanted to congratulate us, and to find out how we had managed to get Steve involved.

A few hours after that visit, I received a message from Steve with a significant development. In essence, it said Julie had contacted him and wanted to sign the IPMN on as cocounsel for the Monfils case. I cried, especially when reading the part where Steve gave Johnny and me credit for Julie's actions. It was soon thereafter that the WIP also partnered with the firm due to their connection with the case through Rey Moore in his appeals process.

I had learned about the legal activity on Rey's behalf when it was reported in the news in 2011. Approximately a year before the firm's involvement, attorneys from the WIP pushed for a new trial for Rey in light of a recantation by James Gilliam. He was the "jailhouse snitch" who had testified against Rey during the original trial, saying he and Rey shared a jail cell, and during this period Rey told him he had helped to beat up Tom Monfils. However, when the authors conducted their research for the Monfils book they interviewed Gilliam and he described a much different scenario. I've added excerpts from the transcripts of that hearing, as told by three witnesses. The legal document they are extracted from is dated January 26, 2012:

(Paragraph 21): Gullickson testified that, during the course of the interview, Gilliam said that Moore had told him in jail that Moore tried to help Monfils on November 21, 1992, and specifically "tried to stop" "the alleged confrontation" of Monfils. In other words, Gullickson understood Gilliam to say during the interview that Moore told Gilliam that he was present when Monfils was confronted by co-workers, but that Moore tried at that time only to help Monfils, not to harm him.

(Paragraph 24): Also at the hearing, Nicholas Schwalbach testified in substance as follows. Schwalbach was a law student working on behalf of Moore through the Innocence Project, with the ultimate goal of attempting to exonerate Moore, when he learned from Gaie that Gilliam "was now saying something different than what he testified to." With two other law students, Schwalbach visited Gilliam in prison, informing Gilliam that they were with the Innocence Project. During the course of the interview, Gilliam said that Moore "had tried to break up the fight and that he did not punch anybody." Gilliam told the students that this account was the same one he had given in his trial testimony." [But of course, it directly contradicted Gilliam's trial testimony.]

(Paragraph 25): Another of the law students who joined in the Innocence Project meeting with Gilliam, Anthony Rios, also testified at the hearing, in part as follows: [Gilliam said that] when he testified at the trial that he was really trying to help [Moore], that he knew [Moore] was innocent,…[H]e said that [Moore] saw a commotion, went over there and tried to break it up. He said that, you know, the whole incident was about drugs, that everybody knew it was about drugs, and he went on for quite some time about how drugs were running through Green Bay and running through the plant from Sheboygan up to Green Bay.

My understanding is that this action was a final attempt by the WIP to help Rey in regard to appealing his conviction. They had not yet dropped his case, and the news that the Minneapolis law firm was now involved came as an enormous relief. They, too, were enthusiastic about the prospect of working with this firm.

This particular circumstance is typical in many wrongful conviction cases, with law firms partnering with Innocence Projects (IP's) across the country. This is beneficial because of the inadequate financial situations of many smaller IP's. These entities are linked to law schools, so much of the staffers consist of a handful of paid staff, made up of lawyers and/or law instructors, as well as law students who donate their time while earning credits. IP's similar to those in Minnesota and Wisconsin are too understaffed to field and assess many of the calls they receive monthly from potential clients. Aside from being able to finance executive director and staff attorney/legal director positions, there are expenses associated with the litigation process. Filing motions, testing DNA and/or other evidence, and hiring expert witnesses, all cost money. Since they don't charge fees to their clients, they rely on state grants and donations from the public to pay for these crucial services. Additional funding provided by law firms contributes to the likelihood of success in any given case.

Johnny was on cloud nine and he immediately began working with Steve on what's called the discovery phase—the period of time in which fact-finding and fact-gathering occurs before a case is brought to trial. In this instance, it was a reevaluation of known facts that were never presented during the trial, and a search for new evidence that may have been overlooked during the original investigation.

They found the facts were there all along, but were blatantly ignored. Aspects inhibiting a fair and unbiased trial, such as ineffective legal counsel, incomplete disclosure of known facts that could have caused a different verdict, and the exploitation of certain witnesses were examined and included in the final analysis of the case. What was ultimately found was a web of deception by an overzealous, but charismatic prosecutor, a corrupt police detective, and a shamed police force. What followed was the manipulation of the facts filtered through the media and an entire community, both of which are still held captive by lies and deceit today.

In addition to collecting information, a legal defense team was created to help out with other aspects of this inquiry needing attention. A decision was made to represent Keith Kutska, the main suspect in the case. Even though he was picked as their sole client, the importance of establishing and substantiating credible new evidence that would be beneficial to all the men was essential. Strong indicators supporting the idea that this death was a suicide became the main focus. The second major hurdle after the legal team was in place was to evaluate whether or not the suicide theory was plausible. When that was accomplished this information could then be presented in a Brown County courtroom, where the case originated, during an evidentiary hearing. The hearing would be administered by the original trial judge, with the defense team requesting a new trial for Kutska.

30

BROADCASTING OUR MISSION

W hile Steve and Johnny oversaw the legal end of things, I kept busy drumming up public support. In addition to bridging communications between Green Bay and Minneapolis, I continued with other related activities. Staying active with our Walks for Truth and Justice, Fighting Bob Fests, and orchestrating a presence of those associated with the Monfils case at future IPMN benefits became more important than ever. Maintaining awareness about the case created a widening interest as the process developed.

My first experience with a television interview took place during the spring of 2012. Jared's friend Erik Stewart offered to produce a segment while taking a video production class at Northwest Community Television (Channel 12) in Crystal, Minnesota. This is a small cable access station that televises local community programming, while offering free video production classes and allowing channel time to residents and organizations in a specified area. From the time Erik first read the Monfils book, he'd expressed a desire to help in some way. So while taking this class, he was able to set up an interview with me and newly hired host Eric Olson. Ironically, this was the first interview Erik Stewart produced. It was also the first interview Eric Olson had been asked to moderate. Being this was also my first shot at being the subject of an interview, we gave each other encouragement before we started filming.

Erik Stewart titled the segment "Seville Disobedience." The video starts with music from a French horn as an image of an off-balance Buick Seville appears onscreen. It then shows Eric Olson and me discussing aspects of the case, my ongoing mission, and reasons for my involvement. This experience gave me insight into how it felt to sit with a camera pointed directly at me. It was exciting but terrifying. My thoughts became a jumbled mess throughout the interview and my entire body shook uncontrollably. I was grateful this video was made available to a limited audience even though I felt Erik Stewart produced an outstanding product.

Denis and I collaborated on an article titled "Walking without Treppa-dation" later in 2014 for a Green Bay monthly publication called *Scene* magazine. For the first time, an article touched on personal and unpleasant characteristics of my childhood, specifically on how I had been bullied. This was something we discussed at length because of the risks involved in putting oneself in the spotlight, especially while immersed in a major controversy like the Monfils case. "I think I can handle myself," I told Denis. "I think of my past as an important aspect of this mission because it explains why I got involved. Plus, it shows why and how I'm able to empathize with what happened to these other victims. And I'm beyond worrying about what people might say."

In a development that fell in line with the many small miracles we witnessed along the way, days before the December 2014 issue was to be published Denis received word that the article was not going to appear in the Green Bay edition, but rather in an expanded issue accessible to readers across the entire state. We were elated. And we were fortunate the article produced no negative feedback aimed at either of us.

A strategic move also prompted by Jared helped to bring the message about this injustice to a global audience. Sometime during the process, Jared described the benefits of social media and stressed the importance of having an online presence. "Great things are starting to happen in this case," he said. "This is becoming a success, and you need to let people know." This made sense, but I was unsure of my ability to maintain these sites considering I was unskilled beyond the basic functions of a computer.

Jared explained standard concepts behind managing social media pages and recommended I start with a basic site called about.me. This site is a single webpage allowing subscribers to post a bio and photo, along with other webpage links with which you are associated. There are countless about.me pages used by people around the world to promote themselves and their interests. The page was easy to navigate and maintain, and a good way for me to get comfortable with having an online presence. It also helped with another difficult task—self-promotion. This concept was a challenge for me because, growing up, I was taught to keep my mouth shut for fear of being humiliated and that exhibiting pride in your accomplishments was bragging.

I don't remember my parents offering many compliments. I do remember something my dad did to let me know he disapproved of my spirited personality. There was always a bounce to my step, no matter where I went—up and down the aisles in church, in the grocery store, at home, and at school. But whenever I walked past my dad, he'd rest the palm of his hand on the top of my head and apply pressure, to lessen the bounce. Then he'd say, "It's more ladylike to maintain a steady stride." Although this angered me, I complied as best I could in the moment. But to this day, I've not mastered that ladylike gait.

Thousands of people from all over the world visited my about.me page. Many of them expressed an interest in my personal mission. I received messages from people who were victimized and wanted to share their experiences. I heard from those looking to be educated, and others who expressed dismay over the subject.

Awareness surged, and I was inspired to start writing a blog with my observations about the Monfils case and other related issues. Jared agreed this was a great move. "Blogs are growing in popularity, and they are considered as a great source of information about anything and everything," he said. "You can then share those posts on your Facebook and Twitter pages so more people can read them." Through my blog, I've connected with people across the globe, and to date it has been read in fifty countries.

Joan Van Houten and I formed a bond that later developed into a partnership. We manage a Facebook page called "The Voice of Innocence," a platform to promote awareness about the Monfils case and wrongful convictions in general, and we invite others to share their experiences. Joan is the brains and technical support behind this page. She also uses it to talk about her personal experience as a family member of someone wrongly incarcerated. She promotes my efforts as well. "I'm so glad someone other than us family members has taken up this cause," she said. "It gives our situation credibility when someone from outside our inner circle speaks out on our behalf."

Joan and I call ourselves *sista flames*, lighting the way to a brighter future for the five men as we administer consciousness about this tragic ordeal. Our personal writings and ongoing activities can be accessed on this site.

An online presence triggered invitations as guests on blog talk radio shows. Friends I met through the about.me site approached me with requests to do interviews. The first was with Suzanne Wigginton. Based in Phoenix, Arizona, her blog talk radio show is called *Souls Aloft*. Our conversation, which aired in June of 2014, centered on the importance of finding and enacting ways to overcome emotional suffering and how I sought to achieve inner peace through my advocacy.

I also met Nina Bingham through about.me. Nina is a life coach and writer. She connected me with a friend of hers named Alex Okoroji, an actress, writer, and host of the blog talk radio show called *The Naked Talk*, based in Lagos, Nigeria. Alex hosted Joan, Johnny, and me in February of 2015. The show focused on the Monfils case and the challenges of dealing with the wrongful conviction of a loved one. Alex invited us back for a follow-up interview a year later.

The three of us were invited on to a third blog talk radio show based in Charlotte, North Carolina, called *Charlotte View*, which aired in March of 2015. This one was also made possible through Nina. The conversation with hosts Claudia Pureco and

Nina centered on the Monfils case and the emotional turmoil surrounding wrongful convictions.

31

COUP D'*ÉTAT* OF SORTS

As the legal process evolved, Johnny and I occasionally met with Steve to get updates on the latest developments. Steve typically recited a litany of tasks yet to be completed and problems he was dealing with. At one point he had experienced major resistance from a private lawyer associated with the Monfils case. The lawyer refused to release the two primary pieces of evidence–the rope and the weight, for the firm to have them examined. The firm eventually won that battle, but the task of investigating and obtaining necessary evidence and information along the way proved to be demanding.

To balance things out, Steve countered his challenges with what had been accomplished since our last visit. I was amazed at the daunting process of reversing a single miscarriage of justice, let alone one compounded by five additional individuals. There were times when we left Steve's office with thoughts of doom and gloom and a hopeless outlook on ever seeing a favorable ending to the insanity. But those feelings always provided us with a deep appreciation of having Steve on our side. His compassion, attention to detail, and obvious capabilities, along with the help of those who eventually came on board, relieved us of the heavy burden we had carried on our own for so long.

Johnny and I also understood how lucky we were, that there had been no discussion of monetary compensation for the hard work the firm was providing. More astounding was the fact that over time, Steve had petitioned the help of numerous fellow

Minnesota pro bono attorneys also guided by a strong code of ethics and not bound by their pocketbooks. These attorneys, along with additional ones from Wisconsin, eventually supplied ample representation for all five men. Since the case originated in Wisconsin, it was helpful to hire attorneys from that state to work in sync with the ones in Minnesota.

What was happening was a miracle. For once, attorneys representing the men were hand-picked for their credibility, honesty, compassion, and level of competency. They are, by far, the best representation the men have ever had. But when Steve talked to us one day about having to hire expensive experts to testify in court, Johnny and I grew concerned. We had no idea where these funds were going to come from, and we feared the legal process might come to a halt.

A few days after this meeting, Johnny and I sat at my house discussing Steve's proposal. Johnny was always helpful in explaining the why's and how's of the process. "These experts are crucial to us and to the case because they can evaluate the evidence, like the autopsy report and the knots on the rope and weight," Johnny said. "They will give credence to the evidence at hand. I think Steve is also planning to hire an expert to assess the lawyers who misrepresented these men."

Explaining this, however, caused a resurgence of ongoing frustrations in a growing list of things deeply troubling my friend. "So many facets of this case were never addressed and those lawyers sat on their pompous asses and did nothing," Johnny said. "They should have been jumping out of their seats objecting to everything put forth by the DA during that trial! And now the victims have to endure more bureaucracy because of the inadequate representation they received. I've seen how slowly the judicial wheels grind and this case will require vast amounts of time and resources because of the number of defendants involved."

We had talked briefly with Steve about fundraising efforts, but Johnny and I knew this could take time to organize. We needed funds now. Out of his frustration, Johnny came up with a daring idea. "What would you say if we jump-started the fundraising process?" he asked.

"How do you mean?" I said.

"Well, in the military we have a saying. It's called coup d'état. In military terms, it has to do with overthrowing, or a sudden forced seizure, usually instigated by a small group," he said.

"Okay?" I said. "How is this relevant to what we are trying to do?"

"It's simple," he said. "What if we plopped some dough-re-mi on to Steve's desk and see what happens? Let's seize this opportunity and get the ball rolling."

I thought about it for a moment. "The idea is tempting but I don't know if Mike will go for it," I said. "We are talking about a lot of money."

"Mike's a generous guy, and I know you can talk him into anything," Johnny teased. "I tell you what, let's each talk to our spouses and see what they say."

"Fair enough," I said.

I broached the subject with Mike that evening. "Sleep on it before you give me an answer," I said. "But Johnny has a good point. It will take too much time to organize some type of event, and Steve is ready to move on this now."

I'll never forget the look on Mike's face when he agreed to it the next morning, or how he said, "I cannot think of a reason not to." This still makes me teary-eyed.

Linda's answer was similar, and later on in the day I contacted Steve to see if Johnny and I could stop by his office for a few minutes. "We can't stay for lunch," I said. "This is strictly business."

We met Steve by the reception desk, and he again asked for a conference room. "This won't take long," I said. "Only a few minutes." After entering the room, and without sitting down, Johnny and I handed over two checks. It took only a brief discussion regarding his acceptance of them before we exited the room. Steve walked us over to the elevator, and as the doors closed we saw him run into Pam and give the checks to her.

What happened afterward was unbelievable. When the WIP caught wind of our contribution, they responded by contributing funds of their own and the following week, the firm approved significant funds via the pro bono department. The case was back on track for the time being, but the matter of additional funding

143

still loomed. However, we had literally bought some time to figure things out until we could come up with a fundraising idea.

32

SOLICITING FUNDS

When the slightest hint of warm weather arrives in Minnesota, Johnny rescues from storage his bright yellow classic car, a 1934 Ford three-window coupe. He's proud of his lemony wonder, with its dark painted stripes tracing the fine lines on both sides and a purple heart sitting on the top right side of the rear trunk door. He earned this medal while serving in Vietnam. He'd take me for rides sometimes while we brainstormed and I'd chuckle at the stares we would get from other motorists.

Johnny drove over one sunny day to again discuss fundraising options. This time we sat in my dining room admiring the car. A light bulb flicked on in his head. "How about hosting a car show and using that platform to raise money?" he said. "I'm a member of the MSRA (Minnesota Street Rod Association) and I have friends with classic cars that love to be in shows. They might even be interested in helping us plan this kind of a shindig."

I didn't know much about car shows, but figured what the hell. However, I saw one big problem. "Who's going to donate money to us?" I asked. "We will need to come up with a legitimate organization that people feel comfortable giving money to."

"Why not ask Erika at the IPMN?" Johnny said. "Maybe they will partner with us."

"It's a great idea," I said. "Let's make some inquiries first to see if this is plausible." After some thought, we developed a plan of attack and hit the pavement.

We drove to a place Johnny knew of called Route 65 Classics, a nearby consignment shop for classic cars. We talked to Sue Stang, the general manager, about our predicament and shared our vision to highlight stories about exonerees while collecting funds through car entry fees and donations from spectators. She was interested so we set a tentative date for the event. We then held a meeting with Erika, Audrey, and Steve. We defined two important aspects of this event: 1) raise funds and 2) educate the audience about wrongful convictions. Our pitch was unanimously agreed upon. We decided we'd do the bulk of the work, with the project lending their name and participation on the day of the show.

Afterward, Mike and I attended some car shows to get a feel for how they were organized and to find either a band or a DJ to provide music. We found Chuck Brost, a DJ we liked who was willing to charge a reasonable fee. Then at a planning meeting with our newly formed committee, we gave this event a name. We called it Hotrod Breakout: Benefit for the Innocence Project of Minnesota.

Prior to the first show, I contacted our local Blaine paper, *Life*, a free weekly circular with a potential audience of approximately sixty-one thousand Blaine residents. For the interview I offered to coordinate with two exonerees who would be at the show, Audrey Edmunds and Damon Thibodeaux. A few days later, staff writer Eric Hagen responded and we set a date for the interview.

Eric looked to be in his thirties. He did not appear to be desensitized or cynical toward this topic, which was always a concern of mine because of the negative spin inserted into the Monfils story in Green Bay.

Eric placed a handheld tape recorder on the coffee table. He looked at Audrey and Damon. "Is it okay to have this going during the interview?" he asked. He was absorbed and visibly moved by his subjects and the horrific stories they shared. In addition to having the recorder going, he scribbled notes on a notepad, intent on capturing every last detail. He took statements from me and Johnny and he used Johnny's classic car as a backdrop for a photo to go with the article.

The following week, the story appeared on the front page. The headline read, "Blaine Residents Host Car Show for Those Exonerated." The article was extensive, filling the front page plus an additional full interior page. Eric had done us a great service by placing most of the emphasis on Audrey and Damon.

Many who attended this event were unaware of the organization and its mission. Some expressed concern over the idea of wrongful convictions and a handful of attendees shared personal related stories. But our efforts didn't prompt large crowds or big donations. The first year we raised $2,600. For each successive show we averaged about the same amount, but for the fourth and final show the total amount of donations dropped drastically to just over $1,000.

Our third and fourth shows were successful in how we presented information. Panel discussions with the IPMN staff, the exonerees, and advocates for the wrongfully convicted brought favorable reviews, one of which came from the mayor of North Branch, Kirsten Kennedy. Another couple reacted to one of the discussions by making a rather large donation. But overall the events failed to solicit adequate attendance and donations, no matter how much time and effort we put into them. So in 2016, Hotrod Breakout saw its last show.

33

LEGAL WOES FOR THE OPPOSITION

Halloween, October 31, 2014. A fitting day to illustrate an unearthing of ghosts still lurking through the halls of the Brown County Courthouse. Finally, twenty-one months of effort put forth by a dedicated legal defense team came to fruition when they filed a 152-page motion, more than one hundred exhibits, and several affidavits in Brown County requesting an evidentiary hearing for Keith Kutska. Close to twenty years later, this small Midwest town was thrust back into legal upheaval.

There was a flurry of news reports on local TV stations and in print. One Green Bay *Press-Gazette* headline read:

"Defense: Monfils Death a Suicide. New Legal Team Seeks to Have Conspiracy Conviction Thrown Out."

When this motion was filed, Johnny and I took great satisfaction in knowing we had played a monumental role in its inception. The families were hopeful. We all felt great about it because there was real progress being made. And our miracle was a kick in the legal shins for Brown County. They most likely never expected we'd get this far or that this case would actually make it back into the courts. But there it was. I imagined the clambering behind closed doors to keep their wits about them because the further this moved forward, the more media attention they'd receive. There'd be no escaping public scrutiny or the tough questions that followed. And it'd be a cold day in hell before those questions stopped. This was no longer merely a movement of family members, close friends, and two crusaders from Minnesota. This motion was spearheaded by a respectable law firm armed with an unrelenting dedication and ability to keep on keeping on.

The main points listed are directly from the original 152-page brief, and are as follows:

- Defense counsel provided ineffective assistance by conceding the State's homicide theory without consulting an independent forensic pathologist and investigating the evidence of suicide.
- The State denied Mr. Kutska due process by relying on erroneous forensic pathology, and perjured fact witness testimony.
- Mr. Kutska has presented "sufficient reason" for this motion.
- The court should vacate this conviction in the interests of justice.

These excerpts are taken from this same document. They reveal major aspects of a failed investigation in a massively flawed case:

> At approximately 7:42 a.m. on November 21, 1992, Tom Monfils—despondent, shamed, and angry—left his work area at the James River Paper Mill and walked toward an entrance of a nearby airlock passageway. As he neared the airlock, he picked up a 49 lb. weight and proceeded through the airlock. He then entered a storage area where his jump rope was hanging on a railing. With both the rope and weight in hand, Monfils walked to a large vat containing approximately 20,000 gallons of liquid. There, he climbed the steps to the top of the vat, tied one end of the rope around his neck and the other end to the weight, and

entered the vat where he suffered traumatic injuries and died from drowning in the liquid.

After a 2 1/2 year investigation, Kutska, and five other mill workers were convicted of first-degree intentional homicide and sentenced to life in prison for Monfils' death. The prosecution's theory was that after Kutska had learned that Monfils had reported him to the police for stealing a piece of electrical cord from the mill, Kutska fomented "an angry mob" of his "union brothers" that viciously beat Monfils at a water bubbler at approximately 7:45 a.m. and then disposed of his body in the vat at approximately 7:50 a.m. on November 21, 1992. That theory embraced the conclusions of the medical examiner Dr. Helen Young, who concluded that Monfils had been beaten and then placed in the vat where he died.

Dr. Young's homicide determination was, however, erroneous and rested on a series of provably false assumptions, as well as her ignorance regarding the engineering design and operating factors impacting the movement of Monfils' body in the vat. As forensic pathologist, Dr. Mary Ann Sens states in her report, Dr. Young also lacked any scientific or medical basis for reliably and accurately determining that Monfils' death was the result of a homicide and not a suicide. Indeed, there is ample and compelling evidence that Monfils had taken his own life.

Unfortunately, residents and law enforcement officials in Green Bay remained unwilling to appreciate the implications surrounding the firm's findings that support a possible suicide. This first round of filings caused the county to push back... hard. They resisted the notion the case had been mismanaged.

They remained as steadfast as ever in a dying effort to uphold all of these convictions, including Mike Piaskowski's, in spite of his exoneration in a federal court. At every opportunity, John Zakowski defends the biggest case of his career with toxic statements that still fuel a vengeful public. Afterward and in present day, his most vicious attacks are aimed directly at his worst nightmare come true. In reference to the release of Michael Piaskowski he flatly states, Michael Piaskowski "was not exonerated," rather, he was "mistakenly let go" due to a poor appeals argument by the attorney general's office. And in a recent interview he did for a documentary about the Monfils case, Zakowski stated, "People tend to say, 'Well, it's only circumstantial evidence.' Circumstantial evidence is many times stronger."

Euphoria diminished as we waited and waited for a reply from the State. When the State did finally respond, it was as expected. In their response, they argued against every measure of the firm's brief. However, it was again the defense team's turn to have one last say in the matter before a final decision was to be reached. The firm was ready. They filed their reply brief earlier than the allotted time.

34

ADDITIONAL MEDIA CONNECTIONS

Media opportunities in Minneapolis surfaced as legal action pushed through the courts in Green Bay. In 2014, Johnny and I made an important connection at an IPMN benefit. We met reporter Ted Haller, from KMSP Fox 9 news. Ted is an enthusiastic and good-humored individual, and he was the emcee of this event.

Of course, Johnny managed to run into him during the reception. When Ted shared his pursuit of becoming an attorney, Johnny told him about our activities. Ted's interest was piqued. I was nearby, so Johnny called me over for an introduction. We shared our efforts since 2010, which prompted Ted to make an irresistible offer. "I'd like to do a news story about the both of you," he said. "I cannot promise anything, but I think I can convince the station to let me highlight you as the Minnesota link to the Wisconsin case."

"I have been trying for years to engage an interested reporter in the Twin Cities," I said. "If you can make this happen, the folks in Green Bay will finally have their story told, in a meaningful way, unlike the negative coverage they've been accustomed to." Mike Pie was at this event, so we introduced him to Ted also.

Months later, Ted reached out to set up interviews with me and Johnny. He also traveled to Green Bay for additional interviews. While in Green Bay, and to our complete surprise, Ted was granted an on-camera interview with John Zakowski, the former Brown County prosecutor who is currently a judge in the same district.

In April of 2015, an eight-minute story featuring this tragic tale aired in the Minneapolis area. It provided a new perspective on the case by focusing mainly on the struggles of the families, with minimal time devoted to the opposition. This was what many of us had wished for since our involvement. For us, it's always been about the silenced voices affected by this ongoing injustice. We see this topic as something society should be concerned with because wrongful convictions shred the very fabric of our society. It destroys families despite claims by the authorities that their presence is solely to protect and serve.

When I'm asked why wrongful convictions should be a concern for all Americans, my response is simple—because it can happen to any one of us, with no warning or conceivable reason. For decades, innocent citizens who make up our neighborhoods, towns, and cities have been taken from their families and sent to prison with no credible, and sometimes fabricated, evidence, for being poor, uneducated, and *different* or simply for being in the wrong place at the wrong time. Law enforcement sees them as easy targets and convenient scapegoats.

In an e-mail from Ted sometime later, he said our story had been nominated within the media circuit for a Regional Emmy Award and was listed in the investigative crime category. The story didn't win, but he said it was a great honor to be nominated. He expressed gratitude for the opportunity to help people through his reporting. He ended with a touching remark thanking me for being on the front lines of those who help others, which is one of the reasons he is able to cover these kinds of stories. Ted continues to be a valuable resource for us as developments occur.

Another significant connection came about through social media. I ran across a reporter named Mark Saxenmeyer on Facebook. Mark has an extensive background in journalism, working in the past as a reporter in various cities, including Minneapolis and Chicago. Mark left news reporting to delve into producing longer-form stories, like documentaries, that address important, yet rarely covered topics. He decided to form his own visual media production company based in Minneapolis called The Reporter's Inc.

When we finally met in person, Mark asked about the Monfils case. He told me about a related project he was working on that addressed wrongful convictions. "It's a documentary called *The Innocent Convicts*," he said. "I'm working with a Texas Tech student who wanted to do a film about the posthumous exoneration of a former student from the same college. Timothy Cole was wrongfully convicted of rape at the age of twenty-five, but died in prison of an asthma attack before he was exonerated. It's a very tragic story."

Soon after learning about my mission, Mark asked me to write an article for his website in November of 2016 to accompany other information related to the film. It was entitled, "How I Became a Citizen Advocate: Wrongful Conviction of Six Wisconsin Men Captured My Attention, Changed My Life." Because of that article, I became acquainted with the film's director, Okoruwa (Ossy) Osagie Nations. Both Mark and Ossy showed interest in adding the Monfils case to the film. In March of 2016, Mark drove his film crew over to Green Bay for a week of conducting interviews for the project. And in September of that same year, Johnny, Steve, North Dakota pathologist Dr. Mary Ann Sens, and me—key advocates for this case—were interviewed as well. This was another boost to give us a wider range of awareness with the film's planned distribution to numerous PBS stations upon completion in 2018.

Another possible connection to this documentary dawned on me in September of 2016. While my about.me page had been active, I remembered seeing a number of Texas Tech students coming through to view my page. This had me curious because of the large number of them visiting almost daily for about a month. Ossy suggested the possibility of these visits coming from law students working with the Innocence Project of Texas who were researching the Timothy Cole story and working to achieve Cole's posthumous exoneration.

I learned about an additional documentary covering this case that is being produced in Madison, Wisconsin, by a father and son team, Michael and Dave Neelsen. The film, *Beyond Human Nature*, is dedicated solely to the Monfils case and delves into the emotional aspects on both sides of this tragedy. According to the film's website, "Beyond Human Nature is about the conflict that erupts between mankind's inherent need to make sense of the world and his limited capacities to do so." I met the Neelsens in 2016 while they were filming at our seventh annual Walk for Truth and Justice. Their documentary, which has been in production since 2014, will be split into multiple segments and may be completed in 2018.

35

SPINS, SLANTS, AND BIASES

The latest attempts in Minneapolis to cover this case were refreshing but formed a distinct contrast in my mind of how slanted most of the news reporting from the Green Bay area was. In regards to our Walks for Truth and Justice, I couldn't say for sure if details were misstated on purpose to lessen our significance, or if the reporters simply lacked sufficient information. Actual video from our speeches was often omitted and, instead, translated with incorrect information. I also noticed inconsistencies with the facts most favorable to our mission. One such instance was when Denis made an announcement in 2012 that Keith Kutska had acquired legal representation by the law firm in Minneapolis. This was stated in the initial news reports, but in later coverage the same stations managed to leave this detail out and, instead, indicated Kutska's legal team was comprised of the WIP and/or the IPMN, and not the large, respectable, and impartial law firm.

In my opinion, these specifics gave the story an immediate negative spin that fueled outrage over a previous client of the WIP, Steven Avery. People were incensed when Avery was exonerated by the WIP in 2007 and then went back to prison two years later for the murder of a young photographer—a case that is currently pending. Even though DNA evidence had clearly eliminated Avery as the perpetrator in the first offense, a sexual assault costing him eighteen years of freedom, the news that he was being charged in a second more heinous crime angered the populace in the state. It resulted in a flood of controversy on social media sites whenever a story about the Monfils case mentioned involvement by either the Minnesota or Wisconsin Innocence Projects.

In my quest to remain optimistic, I thought our message of reasonable doubt about the guilt of these men might eventually start to resonate with the residents of Green Bay as developments and shocking truths about the case surfaced. I hoped the real facts could sway overall opinion. After all, the information was forthcoming from an independent source—the impartial Minneapolis law firm. But when new details did surface, no matter their relevance, the media seemed to downplay them with lesser, more mundane information related to the story. An example of this is in news coverage from 2015. At our fifth Walk, an announcement was made about a possible evidentiary hearing for Keith Kutska. The story was filled with new evidence uncovered by the firm suggesting the death of Monfils was actually a suicide. But as substantial as this information was, it was overshadowed by simultaneous reports covering Kutska's first-ever parole hearing, which resulted in a denial of his release. I've been told most inmates who begin the parole process are typically denied the first time. Still, Keith's misfortune, as opposed to his good fortune, became the bigger, more acceptable news story.

The tide did eventually start to turn, and we did come across two open-minded reporters in Green Bay. On the day of our Walk in 2015, I was interviewed by Raquel Lamal of WGBA NBC 26 in Green Bay a few hours before the event started. This opportunity arose through default. Denis was not available, so I was asked to speak with her instead. Raquel was the first reporter in that town who was open to sharing the real tragedy much like Ted did. For this type of story, I became the likely candidate as an outsider who had taken the time to get to know the families enough to share the depth of the pain they endured. This was also a great outlet to share my message about bullying—an aspect never linked to this case, but one that invaded countless households during the entire investigation. I said outright what I truly believed during that interview, "…that these men and their families had been bullied."

Another opportunity surfaced in April of 2016 after I'd managed to make contact with Rey Moore's family. Rey's daughter, Kayce, asked me if I'd do an interview with Mark Leland, an investigative reporter and weekend co-anchor for WLUK FOX 11 news in Green Bay. Leland was putting together a story about wrongful convictions focusing on a recently exonerated Green Bay man named Mario Victoria Vasquez. Mario had been wrongfully convicted for the sexual assault of a four-year-old child and had served seventeen years for this crime. The piece was approximately eight minutes long and aired in mid-May.

I was eager to be included in this segment because I had become acquainted with Mario while he was still in prison. This was another connection that occurred through my sister Clare who was friends with Mario's ex-wife, Darcy. I had expressed interest in writing to him after talking with both Darcy and Clare about his case. At the time, Mario already had retained legal representation from the WIP, and at one of our Walks I mentioned my communications with Mario to Byron Lichstein. Months later, in January of 2015, I was notified of Mario's exoneration date. His was the first and only exoneration I've witnessed so far.

The FOX 11 segment was a great platform for Mario to share his story. His story needs to be told because of the horrific way the case was investigated and because of how he was treated after his release.

Early in the investigation, Mario wanted to clear himself of suspicion. He asked to be tested for herpes, which the four-year-old victim had developed after the assault. But an old scar found by the examining doctor led him to conclude Mario could have had the disease, which led to Mario's arrest. However, no herpes test was ever performed on Mario. There was no DNA evidence either. Though Mario willingly gave samples of his blood, hair, and saliva for comparison, the nurse who examined the child at the hospital never completed a full exam on the girl, according to court records. These tests should have eliminated Mario right away. Each time he pushed to have his samples tested, he was assured this would be taken care of. It never was. Another contributing factor was testimony from the child. At trial, she'd referred to her perpetrator as "Mario." But what was never revealed was the girl also referred to her uncle as "Mario." Mario's attorney failed to present an expert witness to challenge the child's testimony, something he said he would do in his opening statements to the jury.

It was nearly two decades later when the authorities learned from the victim who her actual abusers were. There were in fact two people, neither of whom was Mario Victoria Vasquez. A hearing was scheduled in light of this new information. But during a second hearing, meant to determine if there was going to be a new trial, the former assistant DA argued they still believed they convicted the right person despite the girl's testimony. However, he also said the state would not be seeking a new trial. This information elicited a puzzled look from the judge overseeing the hearing, who then stated for the record that the victim did identify her abusers and that Mario was not cited as one of them.

After this second hearing, Mario was unexpectedly released from the county jail. It happened that evening at approximately 7:00 p.m. The expectations at the hearing were that he would be released the following week after the paperwork was filed because of the weight of the child's testimony. But unbeknownst to anyone, Mario was sent out into a cold, dark, and blustery night with temperatures in the teens. He lacked adequate clothing or a means to call a relative to pick him up. Mario had no choice but to go back into the county jail to use their phone to call his son. There was no media to hear his side of the story, and no apologies from the authorities who robbed him of seventeen years for one of the worst offenses possible.

What infuriates Mario the most is, even though he has been exonerated, neither of the true perpetrators has been arrested. His concern all along was for the child he refers to as an "angel," and the likelihood that because he was convicted and because the real abusers were family members, the assaults on her continued.

Aside from this aspect, what is equally infuriating for me is twofold: 1) Three months after Mario was convicted a woman filed a complaint against one of the actual perpetrators, the child's uncle. The uncle had denied under oath at Mario's trial that he had herpes. But this woman alleged he had given her the disease during a sexual assault that same year. That evidence remained buried until it was uncovered in 2014 during the investigation of Mario's case by attorneys from the WIP. 2) The main reason I've written as extensively as I have on this case is the fact that the original prosecutor and the former assistant DA at Mario's hearing, also helped to prosecute the Monfils case.

36

ROUSING A NEW GENERATION

An encouraging development borne out of the Monfils case is that we've reached a new generation of supporters. In 2015, I became acquainted with two thirteen-year-olds who support our efforts. One of them contacted me online, which led to a phone conversation. She said she heard about the case in the news and wanted to do a school report on it. While conducting research for her project, she contacted me. "Your name kept popping up, so I wanted to talk to you," she said. I asked her how her peers viewed the case, and she said, "They were sad mostly."

Before school let out for the summer of 2016, she was granted permission from her instructor to invite me into their social studies class. I asked my sister Clare to assist me. We met with about nineteen inquisitive, smart, and open-minded students. We discussed the mission of the Innocence Project and addressed the bullying aspect. We talked about individuals who've been wrongfully convicted and covered some of the pitfalls of wrongful convictions, such as faulty eyewitness identification. We showed them photos of exonerees and asked them to share their impressions of the kind of people they saw. They were amazed at how normal the faces looked.

To make things interesting, we engaged them in two exercises involving eyewitness identification. We asked for their feedback on two actual cases. The first addressed the wrongful conviction of exoneree Ronald Cotton. A brief case summary was read to the class. They learned Cotton was convicted solely on the eyewitness testimony of a rape victim, Jennifer Thompson, a young college student who was assaulted in her apartment, who had presence of mind to study her attacker's face close up. When it came time to identify him in court, Jennifer was 100 percent sure she had picked the right man. As a result of her testimony, Cotton was convicted. He spent eleven years in prison before DNA evidence exonerated him and led the authorities to the real assailant, serving time at the same prison as Cotton for another crime. We showed the class photos of both men. Their jaws dropped at the facial similarities of each of the men. "They could be twins," one of the students said.

In one other exercise the students were asked to identify the correct perpetrator in a case in which a police sketch of the perpetrator was publicized on the news prior to an arrest. In this case the suspect they arrested was guilty but the exercise we were conducting was more about how an innocent person could have easily been arrested if the circumstances had been slightly different. This was a case that hit close to home for my family.

In 1996, US headlines brought news of a horrific bombing in Oklahoma City, Oklahoma. War veteran-turned-American domestic terrorist Timothy McVeigh detonated a truck bomb in front of the Alfred P. Murrah Federal Building in Oklahoma City on April 19, 1995. The blast killed 168 people and wounded well over five hundred. Back then it was classified as the largest terrorist act ever committed on US soil. When the story hit the news, the sketch of the suspect looked a lot like our son, Jared (who was also in the military at the time in another location). When McVeigh was finally caught and his face appeared in news clips, our first impression was that his facial features didn't match the police sketch as well as Jared's did. We wondered if Jared, had he been in that city during the investigation, could've been arrested based on his resemblance to the sketch. To this day I'm haunted by that thought.

When I prepared the latter exercise for the class, I found out from Jared that he had never seen the sketch. When I showed it to him he was shocked by the resemblance to a photo of his from his military days. And for the students at the middle school and at other venues, who are too young to remember the incident from 1995, the majority of them pick my son's military photo over McVeigh's as the one closest in likeness to the image in the police sketch.

The class was surprised at how easy it was to misidentify someone. They were equally concerned when we brought up the idea that when innocent people are convicted the guilty go free, allowing the real criminals to commit additional crimes.

We were quite honored to have met this class and I must admit that they were not the only ones to receive an education that day. Learning about the intuitive nature and basic understanding these students have at their age was refreshing and far outweighed the level of awareness I had back then.

I also met a young man who came to our 2015 Walk with his father. He was shy, and didn't say too much, but his dad told me that when he read the Monfils book, this young man was able to see the flaws in the case and was adamant about supporting this movement. It's hard to measure the effects of these instances, but if they are any indication of what's to come, then it means our message is resonating with an important portion of society—future advocates, future lawyers, and future prosecutors who won't be so quick to convict without adequate and reliable evidence of guilt beyond a reasonable doubt. I see these young people as the brains and compassion behind many future innovations, and I am encouraged that because of their knowledge of this problem, they'll be the ones to reform our judicial system and, hopefully, eliminate wrongful convictions altogether.

37

PRISON VISITS

After a few years of correspondence with the men, I considered visiting them. I felt confident the visits could be positive and upbeat because of the good taking place. I discussed this idea with Mike. He was unsure of me going alone and expressed concern for my general safety. We hear about the riots, violence, and mayhem in prisons from the media, but as Keith once told me, in all his years in prison, he has seen few altercations. Julie Jonas reassured me that visits to prisons are quite safe because of the safeguards in place. However, widespread ignorance about what these places are like causes many of us to exert caution.

Mike offered a quick solution he felt comfortable with that wouldn't restrict my plans. "I'll go with you," he said. We filled out the necessary paperwork and were added to four of the five men's visitor lists. There is a cap of ten to twelve visitors allowed on inmate lists at any given time, and we found out Rey's was already full. To visit him required a different form, allowing a one-time special visit. We'd need to decide on a specific date, so we elected to address this visit later. At the time we had every intention of following through with these visits, but they didn't happen immediately. Life got in the way and it was not until a few years later that I was motivated into action by a good friend.

In December 2014, shortly before I left my part-time job to focus on this cause, Mike and I attended a holiday party for Gentle Transitions employees. These events gave me a chance to share the latest regarding my mission. This year I was bombarded with questions when, right before the party, my boss, Diane, posted the *Scene* magazine article Denis had written, in the employee newsletter.

A conversation I'd had with one of my move managers, Kathleen, who shared an interest in the prison system due to an incarcerated family member, struck a chord. She remarked on something in the article that bothered her. "You stated you've never met the five men," she said. "This troubles me because I understand the importance of them having outside contact. I think you should consider visiting them. You will not regret it."

This caused me to think about my neglect to follow through with visits a couple of years earlier. "Why had we not taken this seriously?" I asked Mike later on. "Because we were too busy, that's why," I said, answering my own question.

It was not an easy process to get on visitor lists. The requirements were painstaking: contact the men, have them request the necessary forms, and mail them to us. We'd receive them, fill them out, and send them back for processing. The men would receive confirmation and let us know if we were approved. Having our names on their lists also made it tough for them to add other visitors. In one instance, our names had been removed and needed to be reinstated. "We simply disregarded the notion we'd inconvenienced them, and we most likely caused them disappointment," I said. "We have to follow through this time."

I initiated the process once again. We decided our first visit would be with Keith Kutska. We eventually received word that we had been approved.

Our visit was on Saturday, February 21, 2015. Mike and I both looked forward to it. However, the worrisome part was the instruction sheet accompanying the visitor forms. There were restrictions regarding dress, conduct, and details that varied from prison to prison. Things like shorts, short skirts, sleeveless and strapless tops, revealing or see-through clothing, spandex, and obscene or profane messages and images on T-shirts were prohibited. And before that day I learned of the advantages of wearing a sports bra. The metal clasps on a regular bra trigger the metal detector and, if you wear one, you will be required to remove it, store it in a paper bag, and shove it down the conveyor belt while going back through the metal detector. A news story I read before this visit described a woman who'd been fitted with a breast prosthesis inside of a regular bra. In spite of her unique circumstance, she was forced to go braless during her prison visit, which caused undue embarrassment. We also learned visitors have three tries to successfully make it through the metal detector before being sent away. Wallets, purses, and cell phones go into tiny lockers, and no items are allowed in the visiting room except a ziplock bag with no more than $20 worth of quarters. The quarters are for vending machines in the visitor lounge. Both visitors and inmates can enjoy refreshments from them but only visitors can make purchases. The two-and-a-half-hour drive there gave us time to mentally prepare for this experience.

We entered the building and were greeted by a guard who explained the process. We felt at ease and even exchanged light banter with him. We put our belongings inside the locker and returned to the metal detector. I recalled stories we'd heard about people who were denied entry due to the high sensitivity of these machines. Partly due to a miracle and a little planning, both Mike and I breezed through with no problems on the first try. The guard even commented on the rarity of that happening.

We proceeded to another entrance leading us outdoors to the next building where our visit would take place. I don't remember feeling especially frightened, even with the loud clanging of the heavy metal doors that unlocked and relocked as we navigated our way to the visitors' lounge. When we finally entered the visitors' lounge, Mike and I took a moment to observe our surroundings. I marveled at how normal everything seemed. The lounge looked similar to many in the free world, except for the long desk off to the side where the prison guard sat. Each table was occupied by one inmate in drab green garb sitting with friends and family members. According to the instruction sheet, as many as twelve people (a mixture of adults and children) could visit at a time. Although the message was clearly stated regarding the limits on making physical contact with an inmate, there were children on their laps and we saw lots of hand-holding. The atmosphere was pleasant. I approached the guard desk to get our table number. "You are at table number seven," the guard said. We sat and took in our surroundings. To pass the time we roughly counted and estimated there were around fifty tables in the lounge. As we visited each of the men on separate occasions during that year we noted minor details like how the number of tables and the size of the lounges varied at each of the prisons. We waited patiently in anticipation of seeing a face only familiar to us through news articles.

After about ten minutes, Keith entered a far door. We recognized him at once and waved when he looked our way. He indicated having to check in with the guard. When he approached us we shook hands and hugged. This felt normal because of how well we had gotten to know each other through letters. We shared a joke as we sat. "It took me longer than usual to get over here because I was eating lunch," Keith said. "But I did a good deed. I gave my brownie to my cell mate." Keith's face was beaming, but he made no effort to hide a sudden outpouring of emotion. His eyes welled up as he shared information about his recent visit with Steve Kaplan. At that time, Steve was making regular visits to see Keith regarding the motion. During their last visit they discussed my presence at Mario's exoneration, which happened to take place on the same day as their visit. Keith said how touched he was about my support on Mario's behalf.

As expected, Keith was not shy and he led a conversation that didn't stop for the next two hours, the maximum time allotted for weekend visits. After we covered current activities in the Monfils case and Mario's exoneration, Mike and Keith talked about fun subjects they both love. Once in a while I was able to get a word in edgewise.

It was hard to believe we were actually sitting there with Keith. To those who know him through news articles, he's seen as a bully. But for those who know him personally—the woman who loves him to this day, a proud son and daughter-in-law who look up to him with respect, and grandchildren who look forward to spending time with him after his release, his character is adamantly defended. Keith was sixty-three years old then. He's educated, with diverse interests including astronomy, history, gardening, and politics. He reads books, newspapers, and keeps up with the latest news and world events, and he is well versed in all subjects that interest him. I enjoyed hearing Keith's observations as we talked about the Monfils case. There was no mistaking it: this man knew exactly what had gone down in that courtroom in 1995 and he was not one to shy away from expressing his views on the subject.

I wanted to make sure this experience was complete, with photos taken of the three of us. I noticed a sign warning us about requesting photos at least thirty minutes prior to the end of a visit. To my dismay, it also said the cost would be charged to the inmate's account. "Don't you worry about that," Keith said. "What else do I have to spend my money on?" He walked over to get the necessary form from another inmate sitting at a small desk. He'd be the one taking the photos. Keith then returned the form and we were summoned within moments to an area with a backdrop depicting eagles soaring in the mountains. I was struck by how drab the scene looked compared to photos our son takes of the Lake Tahoe area, where he lives. The colors on this wall lacked vibrancy with the paint looking faded from exposure to fluorescent lights.

Keith and I were permitted to stand arm in arm, which Mike and I later learned was not permitted at every prison. After the photo was taken, the photographer showed it to us. Keith wasn't smiling, so I chided him. His reply was, "I'm a prisoner and prisoners shouldn't smile."

We laughed, and the three of us posed for a second photo. Again, Keith didn't smile, but neither did Mike. "What am I going to do with the both of you?" I said. "I guess these will have to do," I told the photographer, who smiled at my exasperation.

"I'll have these ready in a few minutes, and bring them to your table," he said. We critiqued the glossy images, which Keith and Mike found acceptable. I shot one last critical glance toward each of them but they appeared more amused than concerned over my woes.

This visit was bittersweet because, within a two-hour span, we'd managed to become the best of friends—carefree, jovial, and close. So close, in fact, that dread set in when the guard stopped by to inform us we had five minutes left. Two hours had gone by in what seemed like minutes. I didn't want to think about having to leave Keith behind. It was during that flicker in time when I understood why it's so hard for family members to visit loved ones in prison. Having to go home without them tears you up inside. Having only met Keith that day and not knowing he even existed until four years ago didn't ease the hardship of having to leave him behind. Being a family member who'd invested an entire lifetime with him must make one feel ten times worse.

In our final moments Keith became thoughtful. "I have to tell you something," he said as he looked at me. "In the span of time between the failed attempt at a new trial for Reynold Moore and the start of the legal proceedings by the law firm, your letters kept me alive." My heart sank as his eyes teared up again. The sight of this big, cuddly teddy bear (as opposed to "a beast of a man") sitting before us was heartbreaking. In a different setting, it was he who provided comfort for his family. Now he was the one in need of the same. I was desperate to provide at least a fraction of that for him until this nightmare came to an end.

This experience was a glaring example of what these injustices do to the strongest of souls. I felt angry at the circumstances, and more determined than ever to see this mission through. And I was forever indebted to Kathleen for stressing the importance of this visit.

We visited the other men throughout 2015 and 2016. Michael Hirn was next. He's the youngest of the six men. He was fifty years old when we met on April 18, 2015. Back when this case was being investigated, he readily took four polygraph tests and passed them all. He also pushed to get the FBI involved in the investigation. Although they did initially get involved, their inquiry was brief. I'm not aware of the reasons for this.

The process was different for this visit. We were categorized as "special visitors" due to Michael's full visitor list. We filled out the necessary form and sent it in. But when we arrived at the prison the form couldn't be located. The guard apologized while acknowledging our long drive. After considerable diligence, he was successful in retrieving it and sent us on our way. In the visitors' lounge we were assigned table number thirty. While we waited we remarked on the difficulties of getting this far. We had scheduled this visit a month ago, but while the paperwork was being processed Michael was transferred to this place and it was lost. Thanks to the assistance of his previous social worker, the process was expedited.

Michael is kind, thoughtful, courteous, and outspoken about the judicial system. Like Keith, he understands how they were wronged. He curbs his anger and focuses on future goals. "I'm serious about my intentions of being an advocate for prison reform once I'm exonerated," he said.

We discussed developments in the case, and talked about his activities in prison. I mentioned the picture he'd sent of the wooden storage unit he'd made in woodshop. "It's obvious you pay a lot of attention to detail," I said. Michael loves the outdoors and he engages in prison sports. At one time, he was umpire for the prison softball league.

Forty minutes into our visit, a guard came to ask if it was okay for two other visitors to join us. Michael's Aunt Marlene and Uncle Terry arrived at the front desk. I had met a few of Michael's closest family members—his son, Tyler, and stepfather, Mike Dalebroux. And each year we receive a Christmas card and newsletter from Michael with a picture of him and Tyler. Mike Dalebroux comes to our Walks and speaks highly of his stepson. Marlene and Terry have shown their support over the years by driving a long distance to visit Michael. When they came into the lounge, Michael introduced us and mentioned my involvement. Marlene thanked and hugged me as tears filled her eyes. Looking at Michael, she remarked, "I don't know how you maintain such a positive attitude under these circumstances." Michael said it was the support from us and many others that kept him strong.

Michael smiled in the photos we'd had taken. Marlene and Terry opted out of engaging in any. "We are waiting until after Michael is released," Marlene said.

We purchased ice cream bars, enjoying them and the few moments we had left before our visit ended. We said our good-byes to Michael and in the lobby, the four of us exchanged contact information. Marlene and Terry were grateful for our visit. We expressed our admiration of their courage.

We visited Reynold Moore on July 11, 2015. Rey, who was sixty-nine years old then, spotted us at table number nine in the visitors' lounge. He waved excitedly, wearing a huge grin. He walked over and embraced us. Hugs were like gold to these men. We felt it each time we met each one of them. Rey's hearty laugh exhibited warmth. The sound of it released the tension I always felt before these visits.

We discussed the disturbance in the courtroom on that fateful day in 1995 when the guilty verdicts were handed down. "Those screams came from my daughter, Kayce," he said. Rey shared how hard it still was for his family to accept what had happened.

Rey is divorced, but stays in touch with his children. Many times he'd ask me to find a way to connect with them. I was successful in 2016 when Kayce responded to my Facebook friend request. We spoke on the phone and later met in person. This was around the same time we both interviewed for the Mark Leland piece about Mario Victoria Vasquez. I, in turn, introduced Kayce to Mario. I also connected Kayce with Mark Saxenmeyer, the journalist producing the *The Innocent Convicts* documentary. Mark asked Kayce to do an interview for his project. She was happy to oblige. Afterward, I sent photos to Rey of Kayce and me, of her with Mario, and of her being interviewed by Mark. Rey expressed his gratitude in a reply letter.

We asked Rey about the original trial and when he felt certain he'd be sent to prison. He said it wasn't until the guilty verdicts were read. His fear became absolute when Mike Piaskowski was found guilty. "The belief among all of us was that Mike Pie would go free since there was no evidence to convict him," said Rey. All along, Rey and his family had a false belief in the integrity of the system and that the truth would prevail and absolve them of any wrongdoing. Instead, a new reality had flooded the courtroom. The betrayal they all felt was beyond belief.

Our final visit was on June 26, 2016, with Michael Johnson, who was then sixty-eight years old. He entered the visitors' lounge. We waved from table number nine. He was all smiles as he approached us. "Bless you, my sister," he said as our eyes met and we shook hands. Many inmates find God during their incarceration but Michael already had long before this ordeal started. He continues to be a steadfast Christian. Reading the Bible daily helps him to cope, to forgive, and to find peace. It helps him to isolate a different existence that truly defines him from the one chosen for him.

We discussed his stepdaughter, Joan Van Houten, and the vision he had years ago. Thinking of Joan and his family brought tears, forcing Michael to reclaim his composure. I spoke about the time in 2010 when Joan described the vision to me. "Joan said both of you thought the woman was her at first, but then changed your minds, believing that she represented me after I became involved in 2009," I said. I fell silent, thinking about the uncertainties we were facing back then and how far we had come since.

Michael spoke of his family with longing—the unfairness, the consequences of being absent from their lives, but somehow knowing God was watching over them and had a plan to reunite them one day. Freedom is a concept each of the men share, a hope to which they desperately cling.

Mike went to purchase drinks for us, while Michael went to the restroom. After both returned, Michael looked down at the palm of his hand and chuckled. He then turned it outward. "I wrote some things down I wanted to talk about but I smeared them when I washed my hands," he said. But the topics we covered triggered his memory, allowing him to recall most of what he'd written. I reassured him the law firm representing Keith Kutska had turned the case on its side to learn everything there was to know about what happened. "They are quite capable," I said. "And they will continue on with this fight for as long as they are needed."

In a 2016 podcast interview with host Lorraine Dmitrovic of *The Ultimate Movies Broadcast*, Joan described evidence that should have been used to prove Michael's innocence. She said during the investigation that Michael had been approached by a local reporter who asked if he knew Tom Monfils. Michael told him he did and that Monfils was a nice guy who brought home-made popcorn into work to share with everyone. He stated, at work, Tom Monfils was known as the "popcorn man." It was later determined Michael was incorrect and that the popcorn man was someone else. Despite these documented facts, the video of this specific conversation with the reporter and Mike's ignorance of who Tom Monfils was, never surfaced during the trial.

Mike and I are grateful for having met Keith and the others, and for the lessons these men have taught us; that in a fast-paced world, it is easy to waste precious time and take everything for granted. That isn't a luxury afforded anyone behind prison walls. Because they thought they could count on their innocence to vindicate them, there's an element of mistrust that develops. And when communicating with outsiders like us, a bond needs to form before trust can be established.

After meeting the five men, I believe those involved in prosecuting the Monfils case had to know these men were not criminals and that they didn't fit a criminal profile. These men had healthy long-term family relationships. They were engaged with their communities. They held good jobs and owned decent homes. It did not make sense for them to throw all that away because a guy made a phone call, and they certainly could not profess their innocence for twenty-three years if telling the truth meant possible freedom. To date, I've not found one person to admit they would either. I feel justified in believing the idea of "the conspiracy of silence" was concocted by law enforcement in this case, and the frenzy was initiated when they realized they were at fault for releasing the tape. But who's going to admit that?

38

REQUEST FOR A NEW TRIAL

Eight months after filing the 152-page motion, Keith was granted an evidentiary hearing to decide if the new evidence warranted a new trial. This was a bittersweet victory for all of us. Although it was a significant step, we knew this action might not produce favorable results. My heart sank when I learned Judge Bayorgeon, the original trial judge from 1995, was coming out of retirement to oversee the proceedings. I was surprised and dismayed to learn it's common for judges to do this. It made more sense to me to have an impartial judge take a fresh look. There was doubt in all our minds that this judge could be objective enough to grant another lengthy trial for Keith Kutska.

I learned a lot about the process that followed. Whenever a convicted person files a motion for post-conviction relief, he/she is required to present new evidence sufficient to warrant a genuine prospect of an acquittal if the case were retried. It takes years, with much of the time eaten up by prosecutors unwilling to admit a mistake was made. They choose instead to fight back. They go to great lengths to explain why the defense has no case and they reason away any new findings. It's a frustrating and exhaustive process not for the impatient or faint of heart.

To give you an overview of the new findings in this case, I've included a rudimentary summarization of the hearing that took place in Green Bay, Wisconsin, on July 7, 8, and 22 of 2015.

REQUEST FOR A NEW TRIAL

Evidentiary Hearing for Keith Kutska, July 8-9, 2015

Day one:

9:00 a.m. – Two objections by DA David Lasee:

1. Discussion about whether to sequester expert witness, attorney Steve Glynn, or allow his presence in courtroom before he testifies. Glynn was then escorted outside.

2. Objection to a last-minute motion admitting testimony for the following day by retired coast guard and former merchant marine George Jansen. Ruling was in favor of the defense.

9:20 a.m. – First witness:

Dr. Mary Ann Sens – Licensed forensic pathologist and chair of pathology for the University of South Dakota. Has been in practice since 1982 and has performed between three thousand and four thousand autopsies (one thousand-plus autopsies involving suicide).

Her conclusion regarding the cause of death of Tom Monfils: "Undetermined"

Condition of the body presented challenges. Evidence proved Tom was alive and still breathing after entering the vat. A police detail sheet was presented showing Dr. Young, the original medical examiner, making a determination shortly after the completion of the autopsy that the death was a homicide and could not have been a suicide. It was the opinion of Dr. Sens that, given the circumstances, Young could not have made that determination because it was impossible to recognize possible injury vs. decomposition due to deterioration, swelling, and discoloration of the body. Also, rapid deterioration of a body happens when submerged in liquid, and then removed. There was no way to determine the exact moment when the death occurred, or if all the premortem injuries listed in the original report were caused before or after entering the vat. A solid conclusion as to a cause of Tom's death could not have been determined based on the autopsy. It required necessary toxicology tests and additional investigation by police, etc. In this case, it might not ever be possible to determine cause of death.

She told DA Lasee she agreed with how Dr. Young conducted the autopsy, but that she would have also weighed the organs. Discussion ensued about how current advances in science allow for different conclusions to be made. DA Lasee pressed that having another expert do an autopsy back then would not have necessarily garnered a different conclusion. Dr. Sens agreed a pathologist might have agreed with Dr. Young regarding which injuries were suffered before death and which were suffered after it. However, Dr. Sens made it clear that all premortem injuries could have been inflicted in the vat.

11:30 a.m. – Second witness:

Attorney Royce Finne – Former assistant DA in Brown County 1977–87. Has focused on criminal cases and did approximately a dozen homicide cases. As an attorney, he has worked on prior cases with Detective Randy Winkler. He was Keith Kutska's first attorney in the Monfils case.

Finne never saw autopsy photos nor consulted a forensic pathologist to challenge the autopsy. He was satisfied with Dr. Young's conclusions and felt the autopsy report was accurate. He believed Tom was murdered. He had no recollection of the other attorneys consulting a forensic pathologist. Was asked about his obligations to his client as defense attorney, and he responded by saying it was to defend his client as best as he could. Finne was shown a number of photos regarding the blade impressions and was asked if he ever brought them to a specialist. He did not. He did not attend all the civil trial depositions even though he was representing Keith. Finne had inquired if police looked to see if there was blood evidence, but hired no experts to review evidence regarding blood and knots. He was not aware of a deal for David Weiner's testimony. In conclusion, he indicated he did the best he could, but did not question coroner's results that a homicide occurred. He believed a beating had occurred, but not by his client. He said all the attorneys believed someone else did it.

Finne told Lasee he felt all the attorneys were competent. He did not investigate suicide. He felt he could not prove this was a suicide and would not be able to find anyone to disprove the autopsy.

1:30 p.m. – Third witness:

Attorney James Connell – Practicing attorney for forty years. He retired in 2014. Did criminal trial work and represented Kutska in post-conviction, and on an appeal.

He hired a private investigator to investigate Randy Winkler, David Weiner, and Brian Kellner. He did not consult or hire any expert witnesses. He knew the body was "mangled" but was not aware of the extent of its decomposition. He felt either Weiner murdered Tom Monfils, or that someone within the mill must have committed the murder. He never agreed with the State's timeline of when the death occurred. He did not believe Weiner's testimony was credible and asked him about a deal. Weiner responded there was none. He thought Weiner knew he was doing something that would get him out early, and he believes Weiner lied at the post-conviction hearing in 1997. Connell did not interview other mill workers regarding a suicide theory and didn't raise the issue of the ineffectiveness of Kutska's trial counsel. He thought all the attorneys were sufficient in their client representation. He went to many of the appeals and there was never any mention of suicide. He concluded Finne did a reasonable or good job in defending Kutska.

Steve brought up a matter involving a Brady rule violation. Under the United States Supreme Court case of Brady v. Maryland (1963), the prosecution must voluntarily disclose material favorable to the defendant in a criminal case that is known by the State. Steve was referring to a letter he argued was not disclosed to the original defense. The letter was from an attorney representing Weiner referring to a deal between

Weiner and the DA's office for his testimony at trial. An objection was raised about its authenticity, and the letter was regarded as hearsay. It wasn't admitted but was placed in the record under an "offer of proof."

2:30 p.m. – Fourth witness:

Attorney Stephen Glynn – Criminal defense attorney for forty-two years in Wisconsin. Helped with post-conviction appeals and has been involved with the Wisconsin Innocence Project. He has worked on approximately forty homicide cases with jury trials and on direct appeals for other serious felonies.

Glynn reviewed both Finne's and Connell's materials in the Monfils case and prepared a report regarding Keith's legal counsel. Larry Lasee objected to the report, which was over-ruled. Lasee then moved to strike related testimony, and it was also overruled.

Glynn testified about the duties of legal counsel to aggressively investigate all avenues of evidence for clients, including retaining experts to create reasonable doubt, especially in homicide cases where life in prison is the most serious penalty allowed under Wisconsin law. He felt failures of the defense counsel undermined the trial and that Kutska, as well as the others, did not receive adequate representation. There was much discussion on a final determination of homicide versus suicide and how the trial could have been different. Counsel should have investigated Tom's mental state, coast guard experience, and family problems. The suicide theory would have explained a lack of blood near the bubbler. A short discussion arose about the prosecution's argument that washing away the blood was effective in ridding the area of any residue. Glynn stated this was not accurate due to the effectiveness of luminal (black light) testing and its capacity to expose residue left behind. Glynn referred to a commonly known acronym among defense lawyers called the SODDI defense (Some Other Dude Did It), and why defense counsel's resort to it was doomed in this case.

DA Lasee objected to Glynn's statement regarding luminal testing. It was stricken from the judge's record.

Glynn stated Kutska's appellate counsel was also negligent and should have brought up the deficiencies of trial counsel. A discussion between DA Lasee and Glynn ensued when Lasee questioned Glynn's conclusions regarding the ineffectiveness of upward of twenty attorneys involved in the entire case. Glynn stood firm in his assessment and added his opinion, which was that had the case been tried differently, "I don't think this case would have resulted in guilty verdicts, and I would bet money on it!"

3:55 p.m. – Fifth witness:

Ardis (Ardie) Kutska – Kutska's former wife.

Ardie testified she and Keith were friends with Verna and Brian Kellner, and were with them at the Fox Den Bar on the evening of the alleged reenactment by her husband, Keith, of a bubbler incident in which the six men allegedly beat up Tom Monfils. Ardie said there was no reenactment. When asked by Steve if she had been asked to testify at the trial, she stated she was not, and was told by Keith's lawyer that no one would believe her. She talked about Brian Kellner's character and said he was "a nice guy, but I think he wanted people to, I don't know, he wanted to make people like him or be important to everybody." Discussion took place about Ardie's many conversations with Keith about the case. Keith first believed Tom took his own life, but was later convinced it was a murder after he read the autopsy report of the forensic pathologist. Keith did not have any idea of who committed the murder.

Hearing concludes for the day.

Day Two:

9:05 a.m. – Sixth witness:

Amanda Williams – Daughter of Verna and Brian Kellner. Also has an older brother, Earl. She could not recall if her parents were going through a divorce or reconciliation during the investigation, but the primary caregiver was her father. She was thirteen years old between the fall of 1994-95, and knew the Kutskas as close family friends. She looked up to Keith as a father figure and recalled when he had colored with her when she was young.

The DA objected to Amanda's testimony about an experience she had with Det. Randy Winkler. This action was overruled, and her description of the incident was as follows:

Amanda recalled being questioned by Winkler after getting off the school bus and spending a few hours with him during the Monfils investigation. She had been asked by him about her knowledge of the case. He asked if she wanted to stay living in the house with her dad or if she would rather live with her mom. She said she felt she was her dad's little girl. When asked if she felt threatened by Winkler, she described physically backing away from him and his immediate and direct advancement toward her. He kept pushing her for answers. Winkler told her if her dad did not cooperate he would be in a lot of trouble. She felt this meant he would go to jail. She was told by her dad to be mindful of whom she talked to and what she said. She described her dad as being stressed about personal problems. The Kellners changed phone numbers a lot and moved. Her dad told her he was being watched by the police, and she said they would see cars sitting outside.

Amanda talked about a woman who appeared at her school one day and introduced herself as a social worker. Amanda said this experience felt weird and that the woman produced no ID. It bothered Amanda that she acted cold. The woman took her to the police station and left her in a room. She was eventually allowed to go home. She later told her dad about it and he fell silent. Amanda explained her dad would get quiet when he was upset. Amanda said her father felt threatened by law enforcement to make certain statements that supported the lead investigators' theory that Monfils was murdered. Kellner finally agreed to make the statements demanded of him. Kellner later said those statements were false.

Judge states he considers all this testimony as inadmissible hearsay.

Amanda told the DA she had shared all this information with Finne. She does not know who the woman was who picked her up, but describes her as having tight curls and glasses. She believed, and still feels, Tom Monfils committed suicide.

DA suggested to Amanda that her life is better because her dad decided to recant his testimony about the Fox Den Bar reenactment and cooperate with defense counsel. Amanda proceeded to lecture the prosecution on the pain that this experience had brought her and how it has **not** made her life better.

9:35 a.m. – Seventh witness:

Attorney John Lundquist – Has practiced law in both Minnesota and Wisconsin for thirty-seven years. He has concentrated on criminal and regulatory defense and is a certified criminal defense specialist. He acts as general counsel at Fredrikson & Byron, PA in Minneapolis. He interviewed Brian Kellner in the fall of 2014.

Before questioning begins, DA objects to Lundquist's testimony as hearsay. Steve argues it is adverse to Kellner's interests and social standing. There is much discussion regarding the relevance and admissibility of Brian's unsigned affidavit. It is accepted.

In February 2014, Lundquist met with Brian Kellner at Mike Piaskowski's house to discuss his statement. Piaskowski was not present during the discussion. Kellner told Lundquist the Fox Den incident did not occur and that it was complete fiction. Lundquist asked Kellner if he would be willing to sign an affidavit regarding their discussion. Kellner said he would. Lundquist prepared the affidavit and was on his way to meet with Kellner in Green Bay to have him sign the document. Just east of Wausau on Highway 29, Lundquist received a phone call informing him Kellner had passed away earlier that day.

DA Lasee asked Lundquist if Kellner had ever seen the pre-pared affidavit. Lundquist replied, "He did not."

10:03 a.m. - Eighth witness:

Cal Monfils - The younger (ten years) brother of the decedent, Tom Monfils.

Cal felt close to his brother and stated they never had a falling out. He looked to Tom with great respect, but said Tom was judg-mental. They shared a room after Tom returned home from four years in the coast guard. Cal talked about Tom's temper and how he would react by going off alone to cool off. He described how his brother would always tie knots. Cal was shown photos of the knots tied to the weight found with Tom's body and described them as knots he saw his brother tie. Cal recalled a conversation he had with Winkler regarding the knots tied around Tom's neck and to the weight. He told Winkler those knots looked like knots his brother would have tied. He said Winkler assured him they had already looked into this, and determined the knots were not Tom's. Cal felt these photos were important because they rep-resented the only evidence the prosecution had. Cal was asked about Tom's marriage, and he said it was "different." He said Tom would do many of the chores at home. Cal did not know if Tom and his wife, Susan, were in marriage counseling. Both their father and uncle had retired from the mill, and Cal knew Tom considered his job a large part of his life.

DA objected to Cal's comments about what he heard from Susan. Steve made an offer of proof. Testimony was allowed to continue.

Cal recalled that shortly after the body was found, Susan had told their (Cal and Tom's) parents she believed Tom committed suicide. He said Susan's statement was known within the family, but the mother thought the idea was silly. Susan also mentioned notes she had found, and Cal felt it was implied they were suicide notes from Tom. At some point after the body was found, Susan had admitted herself into a psychiatric ward and Cal had picked her up after a three-day period. They had gone to make funeral arrangements and were headed to a florist when they heard on the car radio that Tom's body had been found with a rope and weight tied to it. Susan then asked Cal to bring her to the bank instead of the florist. They both went in, and Cal said Susan went to check the safe deposit box. He did not ask her why. There was a lot of media coverage after the body was found, and Cal's mother became the media spokesperson for the family. Susan remained silent. Cal talked to their mother many times about suicide, but she publicly stated Tom would never kill himself. He said their mother is deceased and has been for two years.

The DA asked Cal if he had seen the notes. Cal said he had not. Cal indicated his surprise at the accuracy of the knots tied to the weight and around the neck. He told the DA he was convinced those knots were tied by his brother, and when Susan described the notes, he was sure she was implying that they were suicide notes. Cal testified he wants all possible information on the table.

10:55 a.m. – Ninth witness:

George Jansen – Retired from four years in US Coast Guard. Was active duty from 1969-73, and was involved in search and rescue. He was stationed in various locations including Wisconsin, and was trained in knot tying, rigging, and firearms.

Jansen was asked about coast guard training requirements. They included learning how to tie approximately six types of knots, one of them being the two half-hitch knot which was used as a slip knot for tying up boats. During training they learned to tie all these knots without looking. Jansen proceeded to tie a two half-hitch knot for the court, and made a positive ID of this specific knot in Monfils' autopsy photos. He also identified this same knot as one that was tied on to some common everyday nails (used in construction) that Cal Monfils had found in Tom's home after Tom's death.

The DA asked Jansen if this kind of knot could also be learned in other branches of service, in Boy Scouts, or in merchant marine training. He replied he did not know about the other branches of service, but said he thought it would be taught in the Boy Scouts and Merchant Marines.

11:10 a.m. – Tenth witness:

Steven Stein – Currently works at the former James River Paper Mill (now Georgia Pacific). He started in 1979 and is backtender on paper machine seven. He worked on this same paper machine (seven) with Tom Monfils and knew him for ten years.

Stein recalled Monfils did not have many close friends, and described his behavior as odd or strange. He said Monfils would make fun of others' circumstances. He related the time when his wife gave birth to a premature baby. The Green Bay *Press-Gazette* did an article about it, and Monfils made copies, added derogatory comments, and posted several in various areas of the mill. The union consulted mill management about this and management said they would fire Monfils. Stein asked them not to because Tom had a wife and children to support, and suggested Monfils seek help. Monfils wasn't fired, and Stein believes Monfils was off for a month to get the necessary help. Monfils would talk to Stein about people drowning and how he recovered their bodies, and how they had committed suicide. He would describe types of weights tied to their bodies to commit suicide. Stein said Monfils seemed to have an interest in death and drowning, and they had conversations about how much weight it would take to submerge a body. Stein talked to Winkler about these details, and he also told police he thought Tom committed suicide. At first the police agreed it was possible, but a week later they called it a murder. Stein learned the weight used on Monfils came from the number seven paper machine, and that he saw Monfils handling it before he went missing. He said Monfils was unusually quiet the week before his death. He said Monfils felt his job at the mill was important and was in fact, his life. Rumors surfaced at the mill about Tom's troubled marriage and impending divorce.

Stein recalled the police presence at the mill during the investigation. He said the police didn't hold back their thoughts on what happened and told workers that Monfils was beaten and thrown in the vat. Stein was asked repeatedly by Winkler if he thought Tom was beaten, and he felt pressured by Winkler to say he thought there was a beating. Winkler called Stein a "scumbag" after he refused to say there was a beating. Stein feared for his job. Stein was asked about Detective Frank Pinto, who was working in the mill as an investigator, but said he had no direct communications with him. However, he said mill management told him that his cooperation with police was related to the security of his job. Stein was concerned because he knew of men whose jobs were terminated due to a "lack of cooperation," which meant not saying what police insisted they say. Stein was never told within the mill to not talk to police, and he recalled seeing when the luminal and black lights were used in an attempt to find blood residue.

Stein knew Kellner a long time and became close friends during the last years of Kellner's life, because they worked together on the same job. Kellner told Stein he was troubled by Kellner's statements about the case to police. He also told Stein he sought out emotional and legal counsel. Kellner told Stein his testimony in the case was false, and that he lied on the witness stand because he was afraid of losing his family and his job. He was also concerned about what people would think of him if he changed his story. Kellner told Stein he was having marital problems and was bothered that police had taken his kids out of school. Kellner said he was told this is how easy it is to get to his family.

Stein testified at trial, but felt threatened beforehand. The authorities wanted him to testify that Mike Piaskowski told him that Piaskowski knew what happened. Stein said this information wasn't accurate and that he wouldn't lie. Stein recalled, "An individual basically told me that they could take my life from me—not my life, but my job. Once I wasn't making any money, they could promise I wouldn't have a job in Green Bay. My family would no longer care for me. They wanted me to lie for them is what they wanted, and I refused."

At this hearing, Stein refused to identify the person who threatened him, but said it was an individual involved in the

Monfils case. When asked by the DA why he wouldn't disclose the identity, Stein said it was because, to this day, he still feels threatened that he could wind up like the six men who were convicted. The DA confronted Stein about the fact that even though he didn't lie on the stand, he didn't get fired or lose his family. Stein agreed he did not.

Hearing concludes and will resume on July 22, 2015.

Day three:

9:23 a.m. – Eleventh witness:

Attorney Bruce Bachhuber – Practiced business litigation and family law. He was legal counsel for Sue Monfils, wife of Tom Monfils, in a wrongful death lawsuit against all six of the defendants, and later in a separate civil suit against the Green Bay Police Department regarding the release of the audio tape to Keith Kutska prior to Tom Monfils' disappearance.

Bachhuber had been subpoenaed prior to this hearing by defense counsel to produce Sue Monfils' medical and marriage counseling records. John Lundquist showed the court and Bachhuber a copy of that subpoena. Bachhuber verified receiving the document. He was asked if he brought any of the stated documents with him, and he said he had not. When asked why, he argued they were protected by attorney/client privilege and that he wasn't willing to waive it. Discussion ensued about the relevance of the requested documents in regards to the Monfils case and why they should or should not be provided. Bachhuber added other documents listed on the subpoena were no longer in his possession. He stated he had searched for them, but couldn't locate them. The judge interjected by saying some of the requested documents hadn't been admitted as exhibits at the wrongful death case trial and weren't within the scope of what he'd ordered Bachhuber's firm to produce at the hearing. The documents that Bachhuber did bring were of no relevance to the motion. Bachhuber was dismissed.

9:40 a.m. – Twelfth witness:

Jody Liegeois – Restaurant hostess in Abrams, Wisconsin, 1995-99.

Liegeois said she knew Verna Irish, formerly Verna Kellner, from the restaurant where she was employed because Irish worked at the adjacent gas station and had dined there often. She never met Brian Kellner, but knew he was Irish's ex-husband. She said Keith Kutska was a friend of Liegeois' dad, and that Liegeois had met Keith at the family's home. She followed the trial and was aware of the Irish and Kellner testimony. She had a conversation with Irish about Irish's testimony. Irish had said she was upset because she and Brian Kellner had been forced to lie about the so-called "bar reenactment" in which Kutska had allegedly showed them how Monfils was beaten at the bubbler.

The DA objected to Liegeois' answer. It was overruled.

Liegeois said Irish told her that the investigator in the case forced hers and Brian Kellner's testimony about the reenactment, and that both she and Brian had lied.

The DA objected to the statement about Kellner's testimony. Steve made offer of proof. The statement was allowed.

Liegeois again stated her knowledge that Kellner's testimony was forced by Winkler, but she didn't report it back then because she felt the case was a "done deal." She contacted Steve Kaplan after hearing news reports regarding the first two days of the evidentiary hearing, and the information stating that Irish and Kellner had lied during the trial. She did so because of what she felt she knew.

The DA pressed that Liegeois knew this twenty years ago, but was only coming forth with it now. She answered yes.

9:50 a.m. – Thirteenth witness:

Gary Thyes – Employed as a barber in Green Bay, 1992-95.

Thyes knew Brian Kellner, and cut his hair for a number of years. He knew of Monfils' death and of the ongoing investigation. He said he had to kick detectives out of his shop when they brought in statements for him to sign about comments supposedly made by some of his regular customers who worked at the mill. "They made up stories…they made up what they wanted me to sign," Thyes said. Thyes refused to sign any of the statements. He had conversations with Kellner about detectives threatening to take Kellner's kids away. Kellner also told Thyes he had signed a police statement he later felt bad about signing. They had talked about how Kellner eventually signed the statement when threatened to have his kids taken away. Kellner said he was very upset right after he signed it, and had contacted an attorney about it.

The DA asked if Thyes had ever contacted a defense lawyer. He said he had not and that he didn't start following the recent developments until he read Kellner's obituary (in 2014). Furthermore, he didn't contact Steve Kaplan until he read about the recent hearings. He also said he didn't know Kellner had tes-tified twice about the reenactment. He said he told Steve Kaplan he could pass a lie detector test in regards to what he knew about Kellner. The DA asked Thyes when his conversation took place with Kellner about signing the statement. He said Kellner had come into the shop shortly after (he signed it) and told him.

10:05 a.m. – Fourteenth witness:

Randy Winkler – Former Green Bay police officer, and detective sergeant. In January of 1994 he became the lead detective for the Monfils case.

Winkler was subpoenaed for this hearing to produce infor-mation about his disability settlement with the police depart-ment, along with other documents. He was shown a copy of the subpoena, and verified having received it. He was asked if he brought documents specified on the subpoena to the hearing. He said he hadn't. When asked why, he stated attorney/client privilege, as well as doctor/patient privilege.

Winkler learned the body was found two days after Monfils went missing, and that it had a rope and weight attached. He stated he wasn't part of the initial police team sent to the mill to investigate, but went the following morning. He was looking for trace evidence—blood, hair, tissue, etc. When Steve asked Winkler about looking for evidence of an act of violence at the mill including near the bubbler, he implied Winkler had found none. But Winkler stated this was incorrect. When Steve asked Winkler to clarify his answer and disclose what evidence he was referring to, Winkler stated matter-of-factly that a body had been found. Steve rephrased his prior comment this time excluding the body as the kind of evidence he was alluding to, and reiterated that there was no evidence found anywhere in the mill. Winkler said this was correct. Winkler didn't recall if luminol was used with black light to search for blood. Winkler believed there was a connection between the 911 call and Monfils' death.

The autopsy was discussed. Winkler didn't recall the names of the police officers present. He was asked if he was aware that Dr. Young didn't believe the death was a suicide. An objection by the prosecution was sustained.

There were repeated objections regarding detail sheets and other documented exhibits Steve produced and showed to Winkler. These were part of the initial investigation, but signed by other officers. The prosecution argued Winkler couldn't speak for those other officers and the defense should call them (officers) to the stand. Steve contended Winkler was the lead detective of a major case and should be well versed in the contents of these documents. Steve pressed that Dr. Young had influenced Winkler's opinion that there had been a beating and that this theory guided his investigation, even though there was no eyewitness or physical evidence to support it. None of these exhibits were admitted. They were placed in the record under an "offer of proof." Steve asked Winkler if the bubbler theory was developed before talking with Brian Kellner. He said yes.

Steve stated the police could never match a blunt object to an injury on Tom's head. Winkler said this was correct. Steve presented a list of nine suspects generated in December of 1992. Winkler verified the list, and that six of the men on it were later charged. The name David Weiner was on the list and Steve stated

Weiner was never charged. Winkler said that was correct. Exhibit was admitted.

Steve stated David Weiner was interviewed on numerous occasions. Winkler said yes. Winkler also said he believed Weiner took a leave of absence from the mill. Asked if Winkler testified that Weiner was an important witness, he said he did not recall. Discussion ensued about Dale Basten and Mike Johnson carrying something heavy. An objection by the DA was overruled.

Steve talked about Tom Monfils' height and weight and the distance from where Monfils was allegedly beaten and the vat. Steve asked if Winkler believed Weiner saw Basten and Johnson carrying the body to the vat. Winkler said yes. Steve discussed the logistics of carrying Monfils' body and expressed the added difficulty of having a rope and heavy weight attached.

When asked if Winkler was interested in who tied the knots, Winkler said "yes." Steve suggested if Monfils had tied the knots, it would lead them to believe he committed suicide. Winkler said "no." He also stated he assumed a beating had taken place. Steve pressed that Winkler never found anyone who said he saw a beating, and Winkler said this was correct. No eyewitnesses? No. Winkler stated he presumed there were witnesses, and that the mill workers were lying or covering up for fellow mill workers. Winkler stated the knots were sent to the crime lab. When asked if Winkler was told the knots should be sent to the coast guard, he said he didn't know. Steve produced an exhibit; a detail sheet from December of 1992 that stated that the knots should be checked by the coast guard or the navy. When Steve asked Winkler if the knots were checked by either branch of service, Winkler said he didn't know and that he never took steps to have them checked. Winkler says he obtained knots that Basten had tied, but didn't remember if they were the same as on the body and said he didn't compare them. Winkler didn't find out if Monfils could have tied the knots, and Winkler stated he didn't know the type of knot on the rope and weight.

Winkler stated he knew Monfils had a skull fracture, but that it had to come from something other than the vat impeller blade. Steve produced autopsy photos of Monfils' skull and of the blade edge impressions. Winkler didn't recall them. He also didn't recall that a dentist made a cast of the skull. He didn't recall the width of the wound in the skull or the width of the impeller blade. Winkler said no object was found to match the skull fracture wound. Steve asked if anyone educated Dr. Young on the shape of the blades, and Winkler said he didn't recall. Steve pressed if any expert had determined what matched the blade, and Winkler said he didn't recall. Steve expressed his lack of understanding of Winkler's inability to remember many of the details of the case, despite recent conversations with reporters and filmmakers about the case.

Detail sheets were discussed. Steve asked Winkler if detail sheets needed to be accurate. Winkler said yes. Winkler stated he determined what went into them and that no one else confirmed their contents. Winkler stated they were critical pieces of information used by the police and prosecutors in criminal cases. Winkler typed up witness interviews on his own typewriter. When asked if Winkler recalled visiting Steve Stein at Stein's home, he said no. Winkler was asked if he conducted surveillance. He replied yes. Were reports written up? Winkler couldn't say. When asked if he had access to tape recorders, he said yes. Were they (tape recorders) ever used in interviews? Winkler said no, by choice. Steve asked if Winkler conducted about two hundred interviews during the Monfils investigation, and Winkler said it was closer to five hundred. Winkler was asked if he did reports for each interview, and Winkler said no. He stated it wasn't always necessary. Steve asked Winkler to describe when they weren't necessary, and Winkler said it was when the content didn't pertain to the case or if the person didn't have any information. Steve asked if any interrogations got heated, and Winkler said no. Steve asked whether anyone who stated he (Winkler) did get angry was lying. Winkler said yes. Steve asked if there was a reward for any arrests and convictions, and Winkler said yes. When asked if it was $75,000, Winkler stated he didn't know. Steve asked if Winkler would tell people there was a reward and he said yes, but added no one said they saw anything.

The Reid Method of Interrogation was discussed. This technique is an accusatory process in which the investigator tells the suspect there is no doubt as to his or her guilt. It is done as a monologue presented by the investigator rather than a question-and-answer format. Winkler stated he was trained in this method. Steve asked how many hours were usually spent to question a witness. Winkler said two to four. Steve asked if it allowed you to lie to the subject, and Winkler said yes. Could you coerce a witness into giving false statements? Winkler said no, but added if witnesses didn't tell him what he wanted, he would do more of an interrogation. Steve asked if the method allowed you to threaten subjects by saying they would lose their jobs or have their kids taken away if they didn't tell you something? Winkler said no. Steve asked if Winkler had interrogated Dale Basten for twelve hours, and Winkler said yes.

Winkler said he was authorized by Oconto County to conduct the investigation. When asked if Verna Irish and Brian Kellner lived there, he said he didn't recall but it was possible. Winkler said he didn't recall if they (Verna and Brian) had children, but he was aware they were going through a divorce. When asked if he was aware that child custody was an issue, he said he didn't. Winkler said he met with Brian Kellner to get information on many suspects and when asked if he documented every interview with Kellner, he said yes. When asked if Winkler was aware that someone claiming to be from child welfare visited the Kellner children, he said he had no knowledge of that. When asked if Winkler remembered Kellner asking him to leave his kids out of it, Winkler said he did not.

Steve presented a nine-page detail sheet regarding a 2.75-hour interview from 1994 between Winkler and Brian Kellner. Winkler asked to read the entire document. Afterward, Steve asked if Winkler noticed in the detail sheet that the Fox Den reenactment incident was not referenced. Winkler said yes. Steve presented an exhibit of the statement Kellner signed, and Winkler verified he had prepared it. Steve noted minor changes made with Kellner's initials; three on one page, one on another, but no substantive changes were made on the document. When asked if Kellner resisted signing the final statement, Winkler said he did not.

Steve asked Winkler if people at the mill told him about Monfils' obsessions with death and drowning, and Winkler denied ever hearing this. Steve asked if Winkler ever heard Susan Monfils say it was possible that her husband committed suicide, and he said he did not. When asked if he ever obtained Monfils' medical records, he said he did not know. Winkler said Monfils' death was ruled a homicide, and that was how it was investigated. Winkler also stated even if Monfils had tied knots, this wouldn't have determined it was a suicide.

Steve asked Winkler if the DA ever made comments to him about a deal for Weiner after Weiner's arrest, and Winkler said no. Steve asked if Winkler recalled Weiner stating he wouldn't cooperate in the Monfils case without a deal, and Winkler said he did not. When Steve showed Winkler a news article containing that statement, Winkler said he still didn't recall. Winkler said he didn't recall visiting Weiner at Oshkosh Correctional to obtain writing samples. Steve then produced a letter from Weiner's lawyer referencing the visit and Winkler's own detail sheet documenting it. When Steve asked Winkler if he hadn't told Weiner during the visit that Weiner's cooperation could improve his position if he cooperated, Winkler said he hadn't. Discussion ensued about a series of letters from an attorney representing Weiner regarding a deal, including a possible reduced sentence for his testimony. Winkler denied any knowledge of them or that Weiner's lawyers contacted the DA's office before the Monfils trial. In fact, Winkler denied having any knowledge of Weiner's case even though he was still working at the police department.

Steve asked about a psychological disability claim Winkler had filed with the department. The DA objected. Steve argued it went to credibility of a lead detective in a homicide case. It was decided five specific documents in question would be entered under seal, and that both sides would have a chance to argue for or against their relevance at a later time.

The DA asked Winkler about his work history. Winkler stated he was employed by the department in 1975. He rose to the rank of detective sergeant and worked on the Monfils case for three years. Winkler stated it was stressful being subjected to the conditions at the mill, and that he was under constant scrutiny by the men there. He said he received a death threat, and he also said people claimed Monfils got what he had coming. There was a great deal of speculation within the community, and suicide was brought up often. The DA asked if Winkler ever promised to give Weiner a deal for his testimony, and he said he had no authority to make deals.

Steve established Winkler had an office at the mill, that the mill made it clear that job retention was based on the workers' willingness to "cooperate with police," and that the office was available to perform interviews. Winkler also clarified that he and other officers brought witnesses to the police station to talk.

In conclusion: Judge Bayorgeon commended Steve on his "diligent" and "amazing" job during this entire hearing, before he admonished him for insinuating a "public servant" (the then- DA Zakowski) lied about a Weiner deal. Bayorgeon stated he had examined all the documentation and could not find anything to suggest a deal was made or that the DA lied about it. He indicated those were serious allegations to be making. He added that specific letters presented at this hearing in regards to such a deal could not support the claim of a deal. He also said it was a twenty-eight-day trial with eighty-one witnesses, and the jury was instructed to consider all witness testimony.

Judge Bayorgeon gave each side time to argue the merits of the sealed documents in writing and to submit briefs on the merits of the motion for post-conviction relief.

On Wednesday, January 13, 2016, the motion for a new trial was denied. Immediately following, a similar appeal was filed in the Wisconsin Court of Appeals. On Wednesday, December 28, 2016 that motion was also denied. The next step was to petition the Wisconsin Supreme Court. On April 10, 2017, that motion was denied.

FINAL THOUGHTS

When I combed through all those old Green Bay *Press-Gazette* newspaper articles covering this case I found the stories interesting and thought provoking. It was surreal to be holding the actual print, but disconcerting to read the same rhetoric that is rampant today. Vicious attacks from some locals regarding the verdicts read:

> Justice has finally been served. Tom Monfils can rest in peace. May the six defendants rot in Hell. I think we all know the man was murdered. If only one or two of these men actually committed the crime, the fact that the rest obviously withheld information that would have convicted them, makes them just as guilty. I think that justice was served.

One person had a different outlook, citing the O. J. Simpson verdict, reached just days prior to the verdicts in the Monfils case.

> On a mountain of evidence, O. J. Simpson walks. On circumstantial, and hearsay evidence, where their main witnesses were one guy who was in prison, and another guy who's all pissed up in a bar, they can convict innocent people.

Although our mission is ongoing, I am encouraged by the momentum we've gained through the increasing number of exonerations on record today. Currently, that number has exceeded two thousand. According to the registry there are now, on average, three exonerations a week across the country. This is especially evident in recent years, with exonerations totaling from eighty-seven in 2013 to as many as 161 in 2016. As that number climbs, so does my hope that the names of these five men will eventually be added.

Johnny states, "It is my belief that we have the best system in the world because of our ability to go back and fix what is broken." His belief is legitimized each time another exoneration occurs. While we don't know for sure how many innocents have been wrongfully convicted, estimates range from 3–10 percent. But we do know if a single person is wrongfully convicted, that's one too many. I'm grateful for programs like *60 Minutes* and *48 Hours* that lend constructive airtime to this problem. Documentaries like *Making a Murderer* and *The Innocent Convicts*, and lengthy investigative news stories revealing details about specific wrongful conviction cases, all contribute to that knowledge as well. In the meantime we as a society can no longer claim ignorance as our awareness is heightened through these outlets. I often hear complaints by the public about the biased slants of these programs. I'm certain the same will be said about this book. But in defense of my book as well as related programming, I ask, "Where was the concern over bias when the individuals portrayed in them were being unlawfully convicted in the first place?"

The fight for Keith and the others continues. The process continues to advance and will soon reach the federal courts. This process is confusing, time consuming, difficult, and requires significant legal assistance. The costs are prohibitive for most. Therefore, many innocent people remain in prison. It is a select few who have the good fortune of being represented by the Innocence Project or by private pro bono lawyers.

Our mission is to see all of the men exonerated. I will continue to do what I can to help achieve that goal. How do the families and the men feel about the events of the past seven years? I am certain that they fully understand there are many who care about and believe in them, that they no longer feel forgotten, and are no longer bereft of hope. And no matter the outcome, they are grateful for an opportunity that many others will never receive.

What is the solution to this devastating problem? For those who simply want to help out in some way, please consider a donation to the organizations that specifically take cases of innocence. There are many out there. Among them is the highly visible and trusted Innocence Project. Chances are you'll find one in your neighborhood or in your state. Dollars to them create financial stability and hope. They rightly claim responsibility for many of the exonerations we hear about. They represent a direct pathway to freedom and they may be the only connection to the outside world for many innocent inmates. Something we often forget is when an innocent person is convicted the guilty party has no obstacles to stop them from committing other crimes. Unfortunately, we are unable to determine how often that happens because many wrongful conviction cases do not gain the necessary attention, which is due in part to Innocence Projects being inadequately funded, preventing them from accepting most requests for help.

I'd like to mention one final matter of concern. People often ask me to get involved in their cases. I do not come from a legal background. This is not my career, nor do I claim to be an expert on the subject. Besides pointing them in the direction of the Innocence Project all I can provide is a blueprint of my process and the knowledge I've gained about wrongful convictions. Through this book and my blog I've simply voiced my opposition to a case I read about, and started from the bottom doing what I could. Anyone can do that and, if you find yourself in a situation with a loved one in prison for a crime he or she did not commit, act immediately. Where do you start? Research the case. Collect data and the legal documents from the case, many of which are public record at the courthouse and the police department. Be aware there are costs involved when collecting some of this information. Get others involved. Pool your talents. Make noise in a constructive way. Do not settle. You'll be met with a lot of grief along the way, but like my friend Byron Lichstein says, "Persistence is key." It will take time, but the effort will be worth it and you will see results. I guarantee you will also see yourself and the world in a whole new light. So, what are you waiting for?

ACKNOWLEDGMENTS

T here are many to thank for the completion of this book. My deepest love and respect goes to my sister Clare for her mentorship for as long as I can remember and for bridging the connection to my involvement in this mission.

Authors, friends, and colleagues, John Gaie and Denis Gullickson deserve recognition for writing *The Monfils Conspiracy* and being the example of what can be accomplished with a little determination. Exoneree Michael Piaskowski is to be commended for his unyielding courage and commitment to helping them with crucial details for their book and also for inspiring me to stay in this fight.

Retired crime scene expert Johnny Johnson afforded me with invaluable assistance to fuel this mission and is the best friend a "housewife" could ever have. Attorney Steve Kaplan became our shining light when he picked up a burdensome torch and took all of us on a wild ride through the complexities of the judicial system. I thank him for his tenacity in proving that truth and justice do go hand in hand. I am indebted to Steve as well for his patience and due diligence in critiquing my transcript.

I thank my incredible husband, Mike, and my talented son, artist and writer Jared Manninen, for their support and ability to recognize the importance of my mission, for their patience during my pursuit of it, and their thoughtful feedback and encouragement to finish this book. I acknowledge Jared also for his assistance with technical support and for the many hours he devoted to helping me transform my words into a conceivable message. My deepest appreciation also goes to Erik Stewart, a family friend we consider to be our other son, for his helpful feedback in critiquing my transcript.

I thank Michelle Brown and Krystle Prashad, and all the folks at Mill City Press for helping me through the daunting task of publishing this important first book.

I warmly applaud my associates at Gentle Transitions and all others I met along the way who came forward to publicize my mission, and offer valuable feedback and reassurance, especially during times of doubt.

I respectfully recognize the priceless financial and legal assistance from Fredrikson & Byron, PA, and the staff and interns at both the Innocence Project of Minnesota and the Wisconsin Innocence Project.

Heartfelt gratitude goes to the families and close friends of the six men for welcoming me with open arms and showing me and the world that love and a promise to never give up hope surpasses all obstacles.

And my sincerest gratitude goes toward five future exonerees: Keith Kutska, Michael Hirn, Reynold Moore, Michael Johnson, and Dale Basten for your friendship, audacity, and inner strength to stay true to yourself. I truly admire your spirit and strong commitment to never sacrifice integrity for freedom. You've taught us all what it means to have a meaningful life, about the power of love, and of the necessity of hope. You have stirred many hearts.

CONNECTING WITH JOAN

*R*eclaiming Lives explains the importance of taking a stand and why we must fight for the things that matter to us. It lends proof that we as individuals have the power to create an atmosphere of change within our judicial system. Using our voices to question the status quo and taking appropriate actions no matter the topic can and will discourage what has become acceptable.

To follow Joan's journey, subscribe to her blog at joantreppa. com. To book a speaking engagement to hear more about her personal experiences and her thoughts on the need for citizen advocacy, contact her through her website at joantreppa.com. She is available for groups large or small.

RESOURCES

National Registry of Exonerations: http://www.law.umich.edu/
special/exoneration/Pages/about.aspx

Center on Wrongful Convictions: http://www.law.north-
western.edu/legalclinic/wrongfulconvictions/

National Institute on Corrections:

http://nicic.gov/statestats/

Amnesty International:

http://www.amnestyusa.org/our-work

Wisconsin Department of Justice:

https://www.doj.state.wi.us/

Wisconsin Department of Corrections:

http://doc.wi.gov/about/parole-commission

False confessions/Alford Plea: http://scholarlycommons.law.
northwestern.edu/cgi/viewcontent.cgi?article=
1005&context=jclc

National Coalition to Abolish the Death Penalty:

http://www.ncadp.org/pages/innocence

Mothers Opposed to Bullying Foundation:
http://www.mothersopposingbullying.org/

INNOCENCE AND PRO BONO ORGANIZATIONS:

Jeffrey Deskovic Foundation: http://www.deskovic.org/

IPMN: http://ipmn.org/

Fredrikson & Byron, PA: http:www.fredlaw.com

WIP: https://law.wisc.edu/fjr/clinicals/ip/

APPEALS:

Rey Moore (2012): https://www.wicourts.gov/ca/opinion/DisplayDocument.pdf?content=pdf&seqNo=77188

State of Wisconsin versus Keith Kutska (full transcript): http://monfilscase.com/wp-content/uploads/2017/02/10-30-14_Keith_Kutska_Motion_for_Retrial-1.pdf

EXONEREES:

Mike "Pie" Piaskowski: https://www.law.umich.edu/special/exoneration/Pages/casedetail.aspx?caseid=4057

Mario Victoria Vasquez: https://www.law.umich.edu/special/exoneration/Pages/casedetail.aspx?caseid=4637

Audrey Edmunds: http://www.law.umich.edu/special/exoneration/Pages/casedetail.aspx?caseid=3201

Fred Saecker:

http://www.innocenceproject.org/cases/fredric-saecker/

Koua Fong Lee:

http://ipmn.org/koua-fong-lee-wrongful-conviction/

Mike Hansen:

http://ipmn.org/michael-hansen-wrongful-conviction/

Damon Thibodeaux:

http://www.innocenceproject.org/cases/damon-thibodeaux

West Memphis Three (Damien Echols):

http://www.westmemphisthreefacts.com

DOCUMENTARIES:

The Syndrome:

http://www.thesyndromefilm.com/

The Innocent Convicts (Minneapolis):

http://www.thereporters.org/project/righting-wrongful-con-
victions/ Beyond Human Nature (Madison):

https://www.beyondhumannature.com/

INTERVIEWS:

Seville Disobedience:

https://www.youtube.com/watch?v=G9lsv0lNxzY

Walking without "Treppa-dation":

http://new.scenenewspaper.com/2014/12/walking-without-
treppa-dation/

Suzanne Wigginton blog radio interview: http://www.
blogtalkradio.com/suzannewigginton/2014/06/19/
follow-your-passions-find-your-purpose-with-joan-treppa

Charlotte View blog radio interview: http://www.blogtalk
radio.com/charlotteview/2015/03/09/charlotte-view-
joan-treppa-the-erin-brockovich-of-the-wrongfully-
convicted-1

Alex Okoroji blog radio interview:

http://www.blogtalkradio.com/thenakedtalk/2015/02/25/a-
voice-for-the-hopeless-w-joan-treppa

Alex Okoroji (second interview): http://www.blogtalkradio.com/
thenakedtalk/2016/01/06/raising-that-voice-of-
innocence-w-guest–joan-treppa

News Articles:

October 29, 1995 *Desert News* (Monfils case):

http://www.deseretnews.com/article/447636/6-MILL-WORK-
ERS-GUILTY-OF-KILLING-INFORMANT.html?pg=all

Blaine Life:

http://abcnewspapers.com/2013/09/17/blaine-residents-
host-car-show-exonerated/

The Reporter's Inc:

http://www.thereporters.org/article/how-i-became-a-
citizen-advocate/

Miscellaneous:

The *Monfils Conspiracy* book:

http://www.sixinnocentmen.org/

Jared Manninen:

http://monfilscase.com/

Voice of Innocence Facebook page: https://www.facebook.com/thevoiceofinnocence?pnref=story

GALLERY

2009 book signing at The Reader's Loft in Green Bay with John Gaie, Clare Martinson, Michael Piaskowski, Joan Treppa and Denis Gullickson

WIP attorney Byron Lichstein speaking at 2011 Walk for Truth and Justice

Images of decedent Tom Monfils, convicted men; Dale Basten, Mike Johnson, Mike Hirn, Rey Moore, Keith Kutska, and exoneree Michael Piaskowski used in 2015 Walk for Truth and Justice

Joan speaking on the Brown County Courthouse steps at the 2016
Walk for Truth and Justice

Supporters at the 2015 Walk for Truth and Justice

IPMN Benefit for Innocence in 2012 with exonerees Koua Fong Lee, Audrey Edmunds, Fred Saecker, Damon Thibodeaux, and Michael Piaskowski

Joan with Damien Echols at the 2012 IPMN Benefit for Innocence

Joan with exoneree Michael Piaskowski at the 2013 IPMN Benefit
for Innocence

Johnny Johnson and Steve Kaplan at the 2013 IPMN Benefit
for Innocence

Joan with exoneree Audrey Edmunds at 2012 IPMN Benefit
for Innocence

Exoneree Michael Hansen at 2015 car show

Six Innocent Men banner with Brown County Courthouse in background. Photo taken in 2014

2015 evidentiary hearing at the Brown County Courthouse

Joan with exoneree Mario Victoria Vasquez in 2015

Joan and Mike visiting Dale Basten at Stanley Correctional on
December 12, 2015

Mike and Joan visiting Keith Kutska at Jackson Correctional on
February 21, 2015

Mike and Joan visiting Michael Hirn at Oakhill Correctional on
April 18, 2015

Mike and Joan visiting Reynold Moore at Oshkosh Correctional on
July 11, 2015

Joan and Mike visiting Michael Johnson at Oakhill Correctional,
June 6, 2016

CPSIA information can be obtained
at www.ICGtesting.com
Printed in the USA
BVOW09s1529190817
492484BV00001B/10/P